# ROCKING HORSES

# ROCKING HORSES

### THE COLLECTOR'S GUIDE TO SELECTING, RESTORING, AND ENJOYING NEW AND VINTAGE ROCKING HORSES

## Tony Stevenson & Eva Marsden

COURAGE BOOKS

AN IMPRINT OF
**RUNNING PRESS**
PHILADELPHIA, PENNSYLVANIA

A QUINTET BOOK

9 8 7 6 5 4 3 2 1
Digit on the right indicates the number of this printing

Library of Congress
Cataloging-in-Publication Number
93-70597

ISBN 1-56138-219-1

This book was designed and produced by
Quintet Publishing Limited
6 Blundell Street
London N7 9BH

Senior Editor: Laura Sandelson
Creative Director: Richard Dewing
Designer: Ian Hunt
Editor: Diana Vowles
Picture Researcher: Anna Briffa
Photographer: Nick Nicholson

Typeset in Great Britain by
Central Southern Typesetters, Eastbourne
Manufactured in Singapore by
Colour Trend
Printed in Hong Kong by
Leefung-Asco Printers Limited

ACKNOWLEDGMENTS

The authors and publisher would like to express
gratitude to Patricia Mullins, author of *The Rocking
Horse*, and Marguerite Fawdry who have contributed
so much to the study of rocking horses. They shared
their archives and knowledge with good humour and
grace.

Thanks also to Sue Russell of Stevenson Brothers for
her valued support and help; Susan Robertson and
Frau Rosemarie Vogelsang who opened their
collections to us; and to the many friends, rocking
horse makers and collectors who supplied information
and photographs.

Published by Courage Books
an imprint of Running Press Book Publishers
125 South Twenty-second Street
Philadelphia, Pennsylvania 19103–4399

# CONTENTS

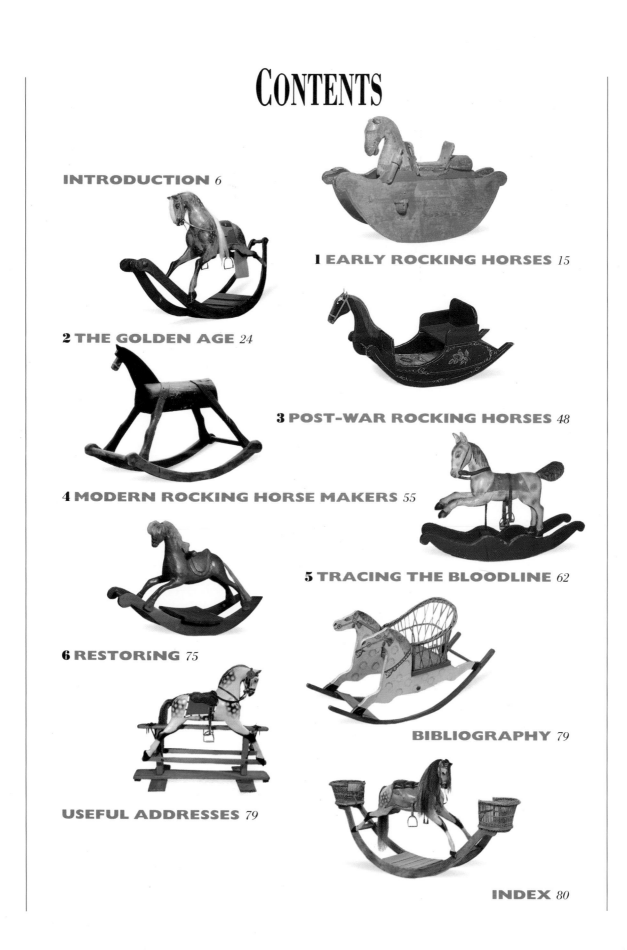

# INTRODUCTION

Rocking horses are eminently collectible because traditionally they have been made to last – and last they do. However, while it is possible to find some horses which are 200 years old, the eternally appealing horses so beloved of the Victorians are more common. These are the antiques of the world of toys and, like any other antique, they can act as a kind of time capsule, bringing to mind memories of places, people, and dreams of past times.

It is astonishing to watch people's reactions when they see a rocking horse. Many different responses are triggered: to some they represent a tangible memory of the stability and security of childhood, while others view them as a work of art. Everybody

## MY ROCKING HORSE – MY PAL

Who is a friend, reliable, steady indeed?
A pal, always there, whenever the need,
Ready for shopping, travelling in mind,
No better friend could anyone find.
My rocking horse, rocking horse steed.

Champing at the bit – ready to stride
The faithful pal, always there to ride.
The mighty charger, made of wood,
My rocking horse knows – it's understood
That after the dreaming, home we'll abide.

There is the moon to visit, even the stars
Maybe China, Spain, also Pluto and Mars.
Travelling o'er the airways, swift and fleet
Our journeys, enchanting, are without bars.

J. M. RILEY MAY 1986

knows of one they knew "once upon a time," and it is a constant amazement to observe the effect they have. The years drop from people's faces, and their expressions become distant as they explore their individual memories.

It is hard to say whether rocking horses are more popular with children than with adults. Certainly there are many, many childless collectors whose passion is due as much to genuine affection for these delightful toys as to thoughts of owning assets that will increase in value. Part of the fascination of collecting them lies in the fact that each horse represents not only the art and skill of its maker, but also the dreams of all of its successive riders.

More than with any other toy, a child establishes a relationship with a rocking horse, the Pegasus companion of fantasy journeys that are all too soon to be overtaken by the more mundane journey through adulthood.

Collecting rocking horses is not just about owning something skillfully made, beautiful to behold, and that may increase in value; it is also a way of tracing historical development. Throughout the centuries, rocking horses have reflected the changing nature of many facets of society. Their design is dictated by the fashions, events, and even the attitudes of the times. The evolution of toy horses parallels social evolution at a level everyone can understand.

In the pre-industrial world, horses were present in all levels of society, as important then as the automobile is now. Feudal serfs worked with them to cultivate the land and transport crops – horses were the only means of transportation available. Small wonder that they figured so prominently in the world of childhood. Children's toys echoed the preoccupations of their parents, whether it was farming, hunting, or war. The poor used "shank's mare," and the better-off rode or traveled in horse-drawn vehicles; armies fought on horseback, and small boys played at being cowboys or cavalry officers.

LEFT **The Charge of the Light Brigade at Balaclava, Crimean War, 1854.** *(The Mansell Collection)*

ABOVE **Morris Dancers with stick horses, 1700s.**

BELOW **Fully carved modern stick horse, by Stevenson Brothers of Kent, England.**

Most rocking horse designs mirrored these aspects of society, as indeed the earliest toy horses had. Stick horses feature in illustrations depicting the performing arts all over the world. They were used by players in widely differing cultures, ranging from the Morris dancers of England to the traditional tableaux of the Chinese. In the same way, young riders of toy horses could, with the ease of imagination, transform a plodding packhorse into a war horse or vice versa, according to their whim at the time. The stance and shape of the rocking horse, however, aimed to assist the imaginative process by echoing the mode of life its designer sought to emulate.

ABOVE **Race for the Great St. Leger Stakes, 1836, painted by J. Pollard. (*The Mansell Collection*)**

BELOW **The quiet demeanor of this group of three small horses on wheeled platforms reflects a quiet way of life. The larger horse was made in Germany c.1920, height 16½ inches, length 17¼ inches. The two smaller horses are c.1940, height 10½ inches, length 11 inches. (*Vogelsang Collection, Germany*)**

Any old rocking horse you find will have been made either by a commercial manufacturer or as a "one off" by amateur and professional woodcarvers. The latter group includes horses made by amateurs from all walks of life, ranging from the frontiersman, with only the natural resources of primitive terrain at his disposal, to the latterday hobbyist who works with varying degrees of expertise. Many old horses were made by carpenters on the estates of rich landowners for the children of the owners.

In the days before the development of sophisticated forms of transportation, craftsmen made use of the indigenous raw materials available to them. There is a centuries-old tradition in mountainous regions of Germany, Italy, Switzerland, France, and Austria for families confined indoors by the severity of the winter weather to employ their time by carving toys from the wood of the alpine forests. The men carved and the women finished the toys with painted decoration in traditional Tyrolean style. These toys were sold at country fairs and at the great Spring Fair at Nuremberg in Bavaria, which, even today, is acknowledged as the toy center of the world. From here the handmade toys were transported and sold all over the world.

World events shaped the development of the toy industry. The Industrial Revolution brought increased prosperity to Britain and an accompanying rise in the demand for luxury items. No longer was the rocking horse the preserve of the children of the landed gentry. The new industrialists, patronizingly dubbed the "nouveau riche" by the old aristocracy,

were building sumptuous mansions and were eager for the trappings of wealth, including large and luxurious rocking horses for their nurseries.

Most of the rocking horses supplied at this time came from long-established German manufacturers which had been exporting their products for some time, but now British makers of wooden toys emerged to challenge them, their products including rocking horses carved to high standards. At the same time, the flood of workers to the new industrial factories generated a demand for toys at the bottom end of the market. This was the beginning of commercial toy manufacture in Britain.

BELOW **Horse with typical alpine painted decoration from Ortisei, Val Gardena,** **Italy, c.1912. *(Pollock's Toy Museum, London)***

Many of the first rocking-horse manufacturers were estate carpenters and cabinetmakers who, like many others, took advantage of the opportunities offered by a stimulated economy to leave their somewhat feudal lifestyle on the estates to set up business in a booming market. By the 1850s George and Joseph Lines had established their company G. & J. Lines of London. Their designs, along with those of Frederick H. Ayres, who came on the scene some 10 years later, were to have a profound influence on many subsequent rocking-horse makers both in Britain and abroad.

So great was the demand for rocking horses that manufacturers soon had to seek ways of increasing their output. British manufacturers looked across the Atlantic to the U.S., and many rocking horses were made there, usually to the style and specification of the contractor, to supplement production. Some inevitably found their way into the home market, and many American horses of this time were, therefore, decidedly British in design and decoration.

European immigration into the United States produced a new breed of manufacturers of wooden horses who drew on an amalgam of international culture and art. Early immigrants, the majority of whom came from Germany, brought with them a rich

ABOVE **Small wooden horse on wheels, unrestored, made for the cheaper end of the** market. *(Stevenson Brothers Collection, Kent, England)*

tradition of woodcarving and an unquenchable optimism. Much of this talent found its way into the flamboyant world of merry-go-round horses, and indeed many rocking-horse makers in the U.S. were

LEFT **Rocking horse made for the children of Robert Stewart by the carpenter on his Canadian estate at Strathgartney in Bonshaw, c.1863.** *(Prince Edward Island Museum, Canada)*

seduced into the more lucrative world of carousel manufacture when the advent of the trolley car brought cheap and easy travel to such meccas of fairground entertainment as Coney Island.

The national enthusiasm for merry-go-round horses had an inevitable impression on rocking-horse makers, and many American rocking horses exhibit some of the showy characteristics of their fairground brethren, although this was confined to the style of decoration rather than the construction. Carousel horses were ornately carved and, because of their exposure to the elements, were made of hardwoods.

An abundance of natural raw materials coupled with a social and economic environment that encouraged innovation empowered craftsmen in young and rapidly developing cultures such as the United States. The cross-fertilization of skills, craftsmanship, and art combined with the ebullience of a young continent produced transformations in the design of rocking horses which have left a lasting impression on the entire industry.

German manufacturers, anxious to remain competitive in both their existing markets and new ones, increased their output and at the same time

ABOVE **This postcard shows an American fairground at** the turn of the century. *(New England Carousel Museum)*

reduced costs by producing skin-covered horses. Only the legs and heads of these horses were carved; the bodies consisted of simple wooden frames padded into the shape of the body with a stuffed animal skin, usually cowhide. This had the double advantage of cutting down on the time-consuming task of carving, and of using less wood, which was still expensive and very heavy. Painted papier-mâché was also used for small toy horses.

The national preoccupation in France was with cycling, so rocking horses were far less popular there than tricycle horses. The materials used again reflected the raw materials most readily available.

LEFT **American horse by an early maker, fashioned in the British style. Origin unknown.** *(The Rocking Horse Gallery, Virginia)*

ABOVE **Piebald skin-covered horse in traditional style mounted on wheeled platform. Made in Germany** **c.1910 by an unknown maker.** *(Vogelsang Collection, Germany)*

Because France was a less afforested country, metal and papier-mâché were often used in manufacture, as they were in some east European countries.

The toy industry has always catered for all levels of society, and the higher the income bracket, the more elaborate the toys. At the more exotic and expensive end of the market, there are some rocking horses, which can be described more appropriately as *objets d'art*, that were produced by sculptors in wood. These rocking horses were usually commissioned by royalty or members of the aristocracy. Patricia Mullins, the renowned expert on the history of toy horses, has tracked down one such horse which was made in 1830 for the young Swedish King Karl XV; it can be seen in the Kungl Lirrustkammaren in Stockholm. Another was the elegant horse made for Lord Grantley in England, exhibiting the stance of the Haute Ecole – High School of Riding – style, which became fashionable in the 17th century. A further example is the fabulous carved cavalry horse in the Royal Palace at Aranjuez in Spain, which was obviously carved for bluebloods who would lead an army into battle.

In Britain more recent royalty has tended to be more down-to-earth in their choice of rocking horses. Queen Victoria favored the traditional dapple gray, while the present queen chose a "Special Extra Carved" Lines Bros. horse for Prince Charles. The Duchess of York kept up the tradition by providing her children with one of the dapple-gray horses made by Stevenson Brothers of Kent.

LEFT **This exquisite example of a 17th-century rocking horse belonged to Lord Grantley and is probably the earliest English example of a fully carved horse. Although it exhibits the stance of the High School of Riding, this was by no means typical of most 17th-century rocking horses. It can be seen in the Victoria and Albert Museum in London, England.** *(The Illustrated London News Picture Library)*

## WHERE TO LOOK FOR OLD HORSES

The days when collectors were asked to dispose of cobweb-covered old rocking horses in attics have almost disappeared, but there are still plenty of opportunities for the keen collector. Apart from the obvious sources – antique shops and toy fairs – many an old horse has been found written off as irretrievable and subsequently skillfully restored. Rocking horses were frequently bought for children's homes, hospitals, and doctor's offices. Having undergone heavy use, such horses are often in dire need of repair and restoration, often beyond the limitations of hard-pressed budgets. Although it might cost you a modern replacement, this can be a way of acquiring an old, and often quite valuable, horse. Rocking horses were also used as props in photographers' studios of old, and although some may have found their way into the auctioneer's hands, more than one has been discovered in the dusty storeroom of a long-established photographic studio.

Most present-day makers also own large collections of old rocking horses, which are mainly kept for the purposes of copying them for reproduction. Once they have served their purposes, it is sometimes possible to persuade the manufacturer to part with the original.

Newspaper advertisements often produce responses from people who have old rocking horses for which they no longer have a use or enough space. They may be only too glad to pass them on to someone who will treasure them.

Before the days of safety regulations for toys, some rocking horses, although attractive, were blatantly unsafe for children. Many of these horses were stored away when they were discovered to cause injury and so have survived better than much-used safer horses.

BELOW **An original F. H. Ayres horse which has been fully restored.**

# EARLY ROCKING HORSES

Europe has a long-standing tradition of toy manufacture, the earliest and most prolific makers undoubtedly being in Germany. Some of the earliest rocking horses known to remain in existence today date from the early 1600s and originated there. Their design was an extension of the rocking cradle, whose action lulled fractious children into feelings of security. In other versions of these early rocking horses, the seat was replaced by a wooden saddle, presumably so that older children could sit astride the horse. These horses sometimes incorporated footrests and a carved wooden holster for a pistol of the type used by horsemen of the day.

Of simple construction, these board-sided horses were made from two semicircles of oak planking, with a rounded log separating them to make a seat for small children. The head of the horse was carved from another block of wood. Reminiscent of the heavy steeds of medieval knights, the body of the horse was often painted on to the board sides in a variety of attitudes. A few remaining 17th-century examples survive, but they are rarely seen outside museum collections. The simplicity and stability of their composition has stood the test of time and is echoed in the design of many modern rocking horses.

BELOW **An early 17th-century board-sided horse with dummy pistol and** **footrests, possibly German, on display at the Museum of London, England.**

**LEFT Carved by the Flemish sculptor Laurent de Vaux (1696–1778), this oak horse is a rare and finely preserved specimen. Length 48 inches. (Museum voor Volkskunde, Ghent, Belgium)**

Small wheeled pull-along horses have been made in Germany for centuries. These tiny log-shaped barrel horses have been popular through the ages, and, unlike their more costly relative the rocking horse, were made more often for children of lesser fortune.

Little horses resembling the small pull-along horses traditionally made by alpine cooperatives were manufactured in 18th-century Britain. Made from scraps of wood, they were of even simpler construction – a log-shaped body fitted with four pole legs, with a rough outline shape for the head. They were small enough for a child to carry or pull along behind. They developed heights of 18 inches and were mounted on wheeled platforms, with the eventual addition of a handle at the back so that they could be used to help the child learn to walk. They were sold at fairs and markets for one penny and were called "Bristol toys."

From these two basic designs new forms which combined the shape of the small barrel horse with the rocking action of the board-sided horse were developed. Whereas the only equine feature of the latter was the head, rocking horses now acquired the basic body shape of the barrel horse, but larger and more sophisticated and incorporating the wooden backrests of the saddles of the board-sided horses. Their appearance was now more realistic than that of their predecessors, with a horsehair mane and tail, some shaping to the legs and hooves, and a well-shaped head with open mouth to take a bit which was attached to a nailed-on bridle. To complete the likeness, they had painted features and saddle.

**BELOW (Right) An original push-along horse from the 19th century. (Left) A modern version styled on the original.**

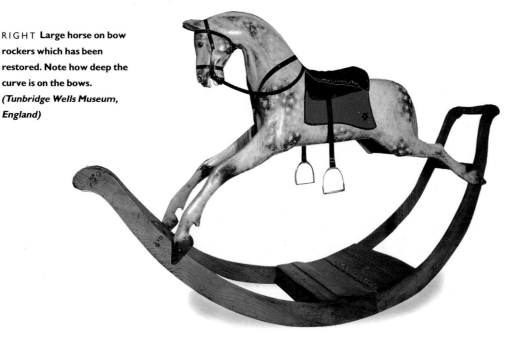

LEFT **Reproduction of a small barrel horse mounted on rockers, copied from an original found in Australia.**

spacers for the bow rockers. The result was a rocking horse which was still quite small – the rockers were only about 2 feet long and the overall height was about 2¼ feet.

These horses became popular with wealthy parents, mainly because of their use as educational toys. At a time when real horses provided the only means of transportation, they offered a relatively safe way of learning the rudiments of riding at an early age – and a convenient one, as they could be ridden in the nursery whatever the weather.

Although rocking horses were produced to attract all children, those built for the offspring of the wealthy classes were larger since they could be easily accommodated in spacious nurseries. With the increase in size came the potential for a more vigorous ride. The bow rockers acquired a scroll at one end to prevent them from overturning, and a further safety measure was to limit the curve of the bow so that it was difficult to over-reach the center of gravity and capsize the horse. From relatively humble beginnings, then, toy horses became not only larger, but also increasingly realistic and sophisticated, some being fully carved and with leather saddles, bridles, and harnesses.

The primitive rocking semicircles were transformed into elegant bow-shaped rockers made of hardwood of a similar shape to the bows used by archers of the time. The rockers were separated by 2 inch-wide planks, and the feet of the horse were attached to these planks, which also acted as

RIGHT **Large horse on bow rockers which has been restored. Note how deep the curve is on the bows. (Tunbridge Wells Museum, England)**

## GERMAN TOY COOPERATIVES

The prosperity of the German toy industry undoubtedly owed much to the national genius for organization. In the early days in alpine regions, the problem of transporting the toys down the mountains was solved by the formation of toy cooperatives. The finished toys would be stored in barns owned by the more affluent families and taken to be sold in Nuremberg in the spring by a toy seller. The mode of transportation was quite primitive – the toys were stacked on a wooden frame, rather like a backpack, and carried down the mountain on the toy-seller's back.

Later, these cooperatives were serviced by agents appointed by the government, known as Verlegers. These agents were more than just salesman; they coordinated the whole operation, traveling extensively, keeping an eye on the competition and the latest trends, and researching the market. This efficient sales and marketing resulted in German manufacturers building up a formidable export market. The Verlegers brought back new designs and samples from overseas manufacturers, which were copied and subsequently sold more cheaply than the originals. The appearance of German rocking horses with English-style bow-shaped rockers replacing the old board-sided models was probably due to this practice.

**ABOVE** A toy seller with his rack of toy horses to be taken down the mountain and sold at the market. *(Tiroler Volkskunstmuseum, Innsbruck, Austria)*

**LEFT** A Tyrolean rocking horse with carved bobbed tail and mane, painted in typically alpine colors. Carved in Ausserfern in the first half of the 19th century. Length 34 inches. *(Tiroler Volkskunstmuseum, Innsbruck, Austria)*

## THE PROBLEMS
## OF BOW ROCKERS

Horses on bow rockers were originally made from solid pieces of wood, but it soon became evident that this presented problems. Such horses were very heavy, and one wonders how many small fingers and toes of children awaiting their turn were damaged by the swaying rockers before the design was changed. Their great weight could also be dangerous if the horse tipped over sideways, as it was possible for them to do. Another drawback was that they were capable of inflicting damage on floors and walls, too, as the heavy rockers ground into floors and the hapless head of the horse gouged holes in walls.

European makers sought to solve the problem by mounting the horse on wheels instead. Although this limited the potential damage, it couldn't have allowed a very exciting ride, especially on larger horses where the young rider's legs didn't reach the ground to push the horse along with the feet. Later versions were mounted on wheeled platforms and

BELOW **A Stevenson Brothers reproduction of a 19th-century push-pull horse with pole.**

BELOW **A very old (c.1750) German wooden horse, height 31 inches. (Vogelsang Collection, Germany)**

were meant either to be pushed or pulled. In the latter case, holes were made in the platform to hold a pole with which to pull the horse.

Besides the production of skin-covered, stuffed horses on frames, a partial solution to the weight of bow rockers was reached by the beginning of the 1800s, when nearly all European horses were made from blocked sections. The body and head were of softwood (usually pine), and the legs and rockers were made from hardwood (commonly beech). This lighter construction was not only much safer, but the wood was less prone to splitting than a solid block.

The problems encountered with bow rockers were never totally overcome despite repeated attempts, particularly in the early 1800s, to find a way of making rocking horses on bow rockers less potentially harmful. Such problems did not detract from their popularity, however, largely because of the esthetic appeal of the elegant curved rockers.

## THE INFLUENCE OF FASHION

The appearance of rocking horses tended to reflect the fashions of the day. Horses were perceived as glamorous creatures, particularly Arab horses, which, with their small ears, were particularly admired. Many of the famous equestrian paintings of the day, therefore, depicted horses with small ears. This might explain why many rocking horses of the same period also had very small ears.

Charles II had a passion for horse racing and the introduction of thoroughbreds meant that equestrian paintings became very popular. However, these painted representations were not true to life and the horses were always depicted with two back hooves almost flat on the ground and the front legs outstretched in the air. Some very old rocking horses dating from this time can be identified by this stance. It wasn't until 1878 when a man named Muybridge began to photograph horses' gaits that artists realised that this stance was unrealistic and both paintings and rocking horses changed.

Later makers made the wooden horses more true to life, and from the early 19th century on, the hooves of galloping horses are turned back to emulate the more lifelike "flying gallop" depicted by artists of the period. The humble rocking horse had been transformed into a racehorse at full gallop. Rockers were now deep and boat-shaped, with curled ends to prevent them from being overturned by over-enthusiastic young riders.

ABOVE **An 18th-century painting by an unknown artist. Notice the small ears on the horse and the way the two hind hooves are touching the ground.**

RIGHT **Late 18th- or early 19th-century rocking horse. Note the small ears and the hind legs on the ground, a stance seen in paintings of the time. (Abby Aldridge Folk Art Center, Virginia)**

RIGHT *Horse Race Derby* **from the 19th century. The horses are in the stretched-out flying gallop. Note how the hind fetlocks are turned back to indicate speed.** *(The Mansell Collection)*

A further facet of 18th-century life was the growth in popularity of riding as a leisure pastime. Interest in the acquisition of equestrian skill had been stimulated by the riding schools in Naples which first appeared during the 16th century. These schools favored a highly stylized manner of riding which came to be known as the "High School of Riding," or *Haute Ecole*. This was reflected in the stance of rocking horses, which show the highly controlled, tightly reined, and haughty attitudes of dressage horses. A straight-legged posture was cultivated by the young riders, with short reins holding the horse's head in and pointing down to one side. An unfortunate side-effect of this position is that the horse's ears, being the first thing to hit a wall if the rider became too exhuberant, were often damaged. Antique horses of this kind can often be seen to have had their ears replaced – probably several times.

In spite of this, the elegant *haute école* design and that of their racy brothers, were universally accepted by 1850.

LEFT **Wooden horse in "collect" posture carved by Andreas Bienz of Basel in 1826.** *(Historisches Museum Basel, Switzerland)*

## COLORING

Many of the early rocking horses were painted white with black spots – and sometimes with spots in other color combinations. There is speculation as to the origin of the spotted horse, some saying it derived from the piebald and spotted ponies of the Romany people. Mullins explores the suggestion that the Spanish breed of Appaloosa was a possible influence. Known as the "Leopard Appaloosa," these horses bore random irregular patches of black on white. A simple and more likely explanation might be that children like bright colors, and spots are easy to apply! The modern British firm of Stevenson Brothers endorses this simpler theory, as it is often asked to paint rocking horses to young customers' own bright specification.

The familiar dapple-gray rocking horses appeared later, in the 19th century. A hypothesis put forward by another English maker, Margaret Spencer, as to the origin of dapple-gray rocking horses is that King George IV, who was heavyset, favored gray horses because the color of the horse blended with his gray riding breeches, making him appear slimmer! Indeed, older grays do adopt a speckled appearance, and George IV did like matched gray carriage horses. This story could well be apocryphal, however, and it is said that the founder of the famous old British firm of rocking-horse manufacturers G. & J. Lines created the dapple design based on the horses depicted in *Horse Fair* by Rosa Bonheur, painted in the early years of the 1850s. The popular dapple was soon adopted elsewhere, so this is not a reliable guide to a rocking horse's country of origin.

Another development in 18th-century rocking horse construction was the use of gesso, which was a white plaster made of powder mixed with rabbit-skin glue. Originally used by artists to dress their canvases before painting, it gave a smooth, more realistic finish when applied to the carved rocking

LEFT **A "Leopard Appaloosa" horse with random spots.**

ABOVE **The Irish cob, which was renowned as an excellent general riding and show horse, has dappling on its coat.**

horse. At the same time, it served the secondary purpose of concealing knots and cracks in the wood. This practice continued into the days when horses were mass-produced, and it doubtless masked some crude workmanship. A form of gesso is still used by manufacturers to this day. Sometimes scrim or cheesecloth was used in conjunction with the gesso, and this further helped to prevent flaws and splits in the wood from becoming evident.

Until about 1870, the bow rockers of British horses were always made of hardwood and usually painted dark green, possibly to give an impression of grass. The rockers on some Scandinavian and European horses often bore highly ornate decoration, sometimes in the form of pastoral and marine scenes painted on the flat piece of wood between the rockers, which was known as the deck. Old American horses featured this kind of embellishment, too, and often the style of decoration can give clues as to the maker.

The Industrial Revolution of the 18th and 19th centuries with its new mechanized manufacturing processes brought about huge sociological and economic changes, which were also to have far-reaching and profound effects on the world of rocking horses. No longer the preserve of the children of the wealthy, rocking horses became a popular toy for children of all classes, helped, no doubt, by the fact that, as yet, there was an absence of electronic entertainment for children, and these delightful toys provided an ideal vehicle for young imaginations to soar.

Over the years, progress brought change, which was again reflected in the world of rocking horses. Trappings became more realistic – the painted-on saddles and bridles of the early horses gave way to leather saddlery, often ornately tooled and adorned with rosettes in the center of the chest and at the top of the bridle on both sides of the head.

LEFT **This horse, with its deep, green-painted bow rockers, is a reproduction of a rocking horse in Pollock's Toy Museum in London. (Stevenson Brothers, Kent, England)**

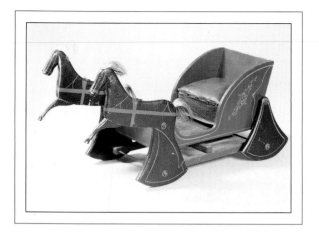

# THE GOLDEN AGE OF ROCKING HORSES 1850 – 1920

CHAPTER 2

The rocking-horse industry boomed in the second half of the 19th century. Manufacturers which were already producing other goods jumped on the bandwagon, and rocking horses were made not only in toy-makers' workshops, but also by companies engaged in the manufacture of baby buggies, furniture, and even sporting goods.

Progress was rapid, and makers everywhere constantly refined and improved their methods of construction. Designs became more varied and innovative, ranging from the tiniest of push- and pull-along horses to the exotic splendor of almost life-size ponies. Designers, eager to cater for all the needs of their young customers, turned their thoughts to finding solutions to the problem of single-rider use – a source of strife in the nursery. Many new designs were obviously aimed at entertaining more than one child at a time, and although the introduction of small seats at the ends of the largest bow rockers had gone some way toward this, these new models were extremely large, some being about 8 feet long.

By the latter half of the 19th century, spurred by the demand, many horses were being imported to Britain from its colonies and the U.S. However, the slender bow rockers proved to be vulnerable to damage in transit, and designers on both sides of the Atlantic tackled the problem. Nowhere was the spirit of invention greater than in America at the end of the 19th century. Patents abounded, and competition to be first in the field was intense.

Although the appeal of rocking horses on elegant bow rockers persisted, the problems inherent in the design persisted. There had been many attempts at creating an alternative design employing many different devices – springs, swings, coils, contraptions using a cantilever system, ratchets, and many others. Many patent applications were made and granted, but the most successful invention was by P. J. Marqua of Cincinatti, Ohio.

## MARQUA'S SAFETY STAND

Patented in January 1880, Marqua's "safety stand" was a vast improvement on traditional rockers from the point of view of both safety and wear and tear on flooring, furniture, and walls. Besides the fact that small fingers and toes were no longer threatened by the rockers, the safety stand offered a more restricted ride since the horse no longer traveled across the floor. Along with this safety stand came a change in the conformation of the rocking horse: the legs lost the spread-out appearance that had been necessary to accommodate the width of the bows and now adopted a more vertical position.

Marqua's new safety stand proved to be very popular, and soon manufacturers throughout the world were offering it as an alternative to the traditional bow rockers. However, although the market for horses on bow rockers was dented, it was never eliminated, because the new stand lacked the graceful lines of its classy predecessor.

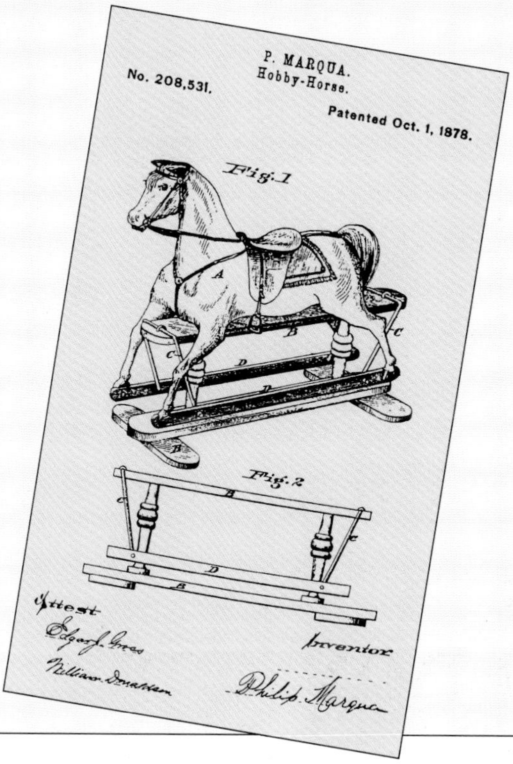

RIGHT **Patent for P. J. Marqua's Safety Stand Hobby Horse.**

P. MARQUA.
Hobby-Horse.
No. 208,531.
Patented Oct. 1, 1878.

Fig. 1

Fig. 2

OPPOSITE **Unusual American double-horse chair rocker c.1880. Note the fine stenciled decoration on the chair and rockers. Height 17 inches, length 35 inches, width 14½ inches.** *(Abby Aldrich Rockefeller Folk Art Center, Virginia)*

BELOW **A fine reproduction of a large Georgian bow rocking horse with chairs** made by Stevenson Brothers of Kent, England. An unusual feature of this horse is that the chairs are made of wickerwork – most reproductions have wooden turned chairs. Length 6¼ feet.

Marqua's new design (see page 25) wasn't without its own flaws, however. The deck of the bow rockers had provided children with a platform from which to mount, but on the swinging stand, which lacked a platform, the side rails (although not intended for this purpose) were often used by children to launch themselves onto the rocking horse. The effect of this was that swing irons were often twisted and needed repair.

In spite of this, the safety stand became more popular than bow rockers. However, horses with bow rockers were and are still made, and it is unlikely

LEFT **Natural wood replica of G. & J. Lines horse and cart, c.1920.**

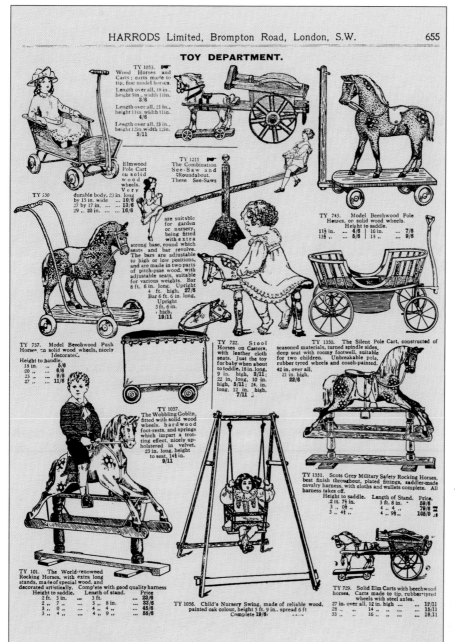

that, from an esthetic point of view, the graceful sweep of the slender rockers will ever be surpassed.

Variations on the swing stand came to include underslung swing stands and spring mechanisms. These were popular because they allowed more flexibility in the design. Without the constraints of having the legs attached to bow rockers, designers could create a wide variety of postures.

In the late 19th and early 20th centuries, the influence of technological advance began to emerge in the character of toy horses. Manufacturers vied with each other to produce innovative designs, and while the rocking horse remained the most popular of toy horses, variations appeared in the form of horse velocipedes, sulkies, ride-in gigs, and novelty items such as gypsy caravans and even farm carts.

## GERMAN MAKERS

The efficient managers of the German toy industry were quick to cash in on the export boom of the 1850s. The five major toy-making centers in Germany circled the town of Nuremberg which, situated on the major Rhine-Danube trading route, had become the main sales and distribution point for the German toy industry:

1.  Oberamergau in the south
2.  Berchestesgaden district in the east (near Salzburg on the Austrian border)
3.  Groden Valley (below Innsbruck) in the southern Tyrol
4.  Central/eastern Germany Thuringian Forest area – mainly in Sonneberg
5.  Erzebirge mountain area (Saxony)

The most prolific manufacturers of rocking horses came from the Thuringian Forest area.

The range, variety, and quantity of rocking horses passing through Nuremberg even in the early part of the 19th century was awesome. Thousands upon thousands of horses were made, some wooden, many skin-covered and stuffed, others of papier-mâché. The bloodline of German rocking horses derived from far and wide, and their stance mirrored all aspects of society. The show ring was echoed by horses on bow rockers with front legs in the air rearing for the jumps, or collected for dressage with one foot stylishly off the ground; German military tradition shone through in the trappings of some horses, and circus horses bedecked with plumes were a popular line.

**BELOW** This little landau pulled by a horse dates from 1900 and comes from Germany. The horse is 18 inches long and 16 inches high and the total length of coach and horse is 51 inches *(Vogelsang Collection, Germany)*

**ABOVE** German skin-covered horse c.1890. Height 28 inches. *(John and Dorothy Woods, England)*

German manufacturers were among the first to change their methods of production to match the increased demand, replacing much of the time-consuming carving, which required skilled craftsmen, with the less labor-intensive processes involved in producing toys from molded cast metal.

Patricia Mullins traced the development of papier-mâché in the toy industry in Germany to two men. It was first introduced in 1805 by Johann Friedrich Müller of Sonneberg, but, although as a raw material it was cheap, working with it could be time-consuming. According to Patricia Mullins, it was not until 1894 that Martin Herdler, another Sonneberg man, who was a sculptor, perfected a papier-mâché which could be poured into molds. Rocking horses made of this material were varnished or covered in gesso, then painted or sometimes covered in plush fabric. Painted versions of papier-mâché rocking horses are fun to collect because of the individuality of the decoration, which is absent in their skin- and fabric-covered brethren. Some horses were made entirely from this material, the legs reinforced with wire. In others, only the body and head were papier-mâché, and wooden legs were inserted into the molded bodies.

Most skin-covered horses were German. They were stuffed with sawdust, wood shavings, or hay, and there was little deviation from the original method in their construction. As a result, it is difficult to distinguish horses from one manufacturer from those of another. All ends of the market were catered for, and around the turn of the century, as an alternative to the expensive calfskin covering of the upmarket models, horses were sold covered in cloth, felt, and plush fabric.

The introduction of a general free-trade licence in 1862 opened the way for merchants and traders to export freely. Many took advantage of this. Although there were dozens of rocking-horse makers in Germany, the most prolific producers and exporters were Beck & Schultz, Carl Jager, F. W. Freitag, and Bauer & Krause. All of these companies had trading agreements with American suppliers like L. H. Mace & Co., Sears, Roebuck & Co., and F. A. O. Schwarz in New York to stock and sell their rocking horses, so the most commonly found skin- and fabric-covered rocking horses in the U.S. are likely to have come from one of these manufacturers.

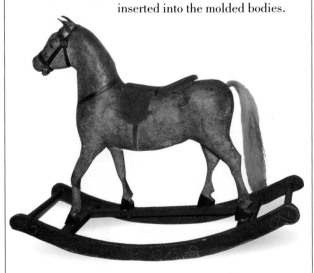

ABOVE **German papier mâché horse c.1850. Height 29 inches, length 30 inches.** *(Vogelsang Collection, Germany)*

ABOVE **German horse covered in brown material, c.1920. Height 26 inches,** **length 25 inches.** *(Vogelsang Collection, Germany)*

These German toy firms kept pace with current innovations. Alongside horses on traditional bow rockers and those on convertible rockers and platforms, toy catalogs illustrated a dazzling array of horse-related novelties: delightful cabriolets (wheeled baby buggies with a little horse trotting in front between shafts, bobbing up and down over a single wheel as the carriage was pushed); sulkies for older children; horses pulling all sorts of different wagons; tricycle horses and velocipedes. Little trotting horses were made, diminutive brothers of larger, popular Trotters known in Germany as

"Traber," which were often mounted on wheeled platforms over bow rockers. The soft toy company of Margarete Steiff, famous for toy animals and credited with the introduction of the first teddy bear, also produced toy horses and donkeys, both on wheels and on shallow bow rockers.

The manufacture of rocking horses in central Europe was by no means confined to Germany, however. Although perhaps not on as large a scale, makers thrived in Austria, Switzerland, and Italy using manufacturing methods similar to those employed elsewhere.

LEFT **Plush-covered rocking horse from the firm of Margarete Steiff of Germany. This model has a well-defined body shape. Height 21 inches, length 20 inches.** *(Vogelsang Collection, Germany)*

OPPOSITE **Characterful skin-covered horse, probably German, c.1900. Mounted on convertible rocker and platform.** *(Musée de Jouets, Poissy, France)*

RIGHT **Novelties from Germany at the beginning of the 20th century. (Der Universal Spielwarn Katalog** *Manfred Rachman Edition Leipzig, 1985)*

ABOVE **A horse made from new materials on sale in New York at the beginning of this century included in L. H. Mace & Co.'s catalog, 1907.** *(Washington Dolls' House and Toy Museum)*

ABOVE **An early 19th-century Viennese skin-covered horse on a wheeled platform base.** *(Salzburg Carolina Augusteum Museum, Austria)*

ABOVE **A small, traditionally decorated push-along horse from the town of** Ortesei, formerly in Austria, now Italy. *(Pollock's Toy Museum, London)*

ABOVE **Horse with carved head and stuffed body on bow rockers from Vienna c.1860.** Jute covering. *(Salzburg Carolina Augusteum Museum, Austria)*

ABOVE **A 20th-century painted wooden horse from** Switzerland. *(Historisches Museum Basel, Switzerland)*

## BRITISH MAKERS

The most popular finish for gessoed horses in Britain was dapple gray. Some skin-covered horses were produced by British makers to satisfy up-scale customers, but these differed from their German counterparts in that calfskin was stretched over the carved body, whereas in German versions only the head and legs were carved.

The reign of Queen Victoria and her consort Prince Albert fueled the boom in rocking-horse production. With nine children to their credit, they set the nation an example of pure and upright family life which was in marked contrast to the habitual dissoluteness of previous reigns. Doubtless the dappled-gray mounts of the royal nursery were instrumental in influencing the rise in popularity of these charming toys, which came to symbolize the stability and endurance of Victorian family life.

Rocking horses made by British manufacturers are more easily identified than German ones because only four main companies dominated the market – F. H. Ayres, G. & J. Lines, Lines Bros. (formed by the sons of Joseph Lines of G. & J. Lines), and J. Collinson & Sons of Liverpool. The oldest-established of these was Collinson, which started making rocking horses in 1836 and is still making them now. Although not the most elegantly carved, Collinson's mounts have never lost their appeal.

In 1851 Queen Victoria visited the workshop of J. Collinson & Sons and expressed a preference for a dapple-gray horse – giving rise to yet another reason for the tremendous popularity of the mottled mounts. From that time until the present day, Collinson has produced mainly dapple-gray rocking horses. The distinctive Collinson design has changed little over the years, and because of this, the company's horses are readily identifiable.

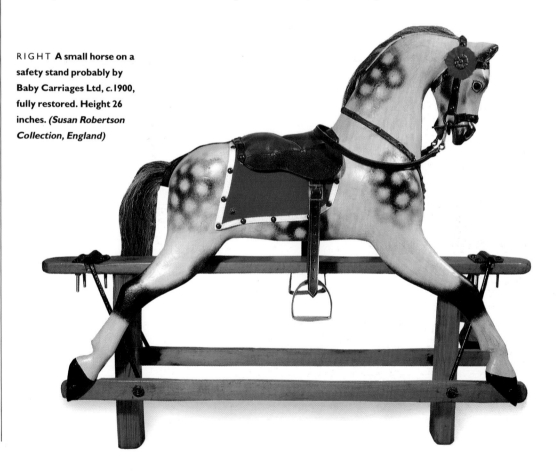

RIGHT **A small horse on a safety stand probably by Baby Carriages Ltd, *c.*1900, fully restored. Height 26 inches.** (*Susan Robertson Collection, England*)

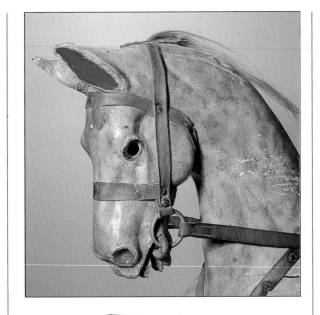

The 1850s saw the beginning of the legendary firm of brothers George and Joseph Lines. Their toy factory became the biggest in Britain, manufacturing rocking horses, display horses, and merry-go-round horses, among other toys. The brothers were good businessmen, and their success was due as much to their sound knowledge of the value of marketing as to the excellence of their products. The elegance of their designs for rocking horses has provided a benchmark for makers up until the present day, and the skill of their carvers was renowned.

G. & J. Lines was enormously successful, turning out thousands of rocking horses until the beginning of World War I. In 1887 the company patented a swing stand, an alternative fashioned on the same principle as Marqua's invention but in reverse, the

ABOVE **The head on this fine "extra carved" example of a G. & J. Lines horse shows the slimly arched neck, which differentiates it from the shorter, fatter necks on Lines Bros. horses. (Stevenson Brothers, Kent, England)**

RIGHT **A Lines Bros. "Hollow Push Horse" on a green base, mounted on steel disk wheels with rubber tires (1937). This little push-along horse was made in three sizes – height to handle 20 inches, 24 inches and 26 inches. (Stevenson Brothers, Kent, England)**

RIGHT **A small, pretty bow rocker, probably a G. & J. Lines horse which has been fully restored. Height 56cm (22in).** *(Susan Robertson Collection, England)*

horse being attached at the belly to a semicircle which swung from irons attached to corner pieces. This had the advantage over Marqua's stand of eliminating damage caused by children using the side-rails as footrests when they climbed on the horse. The new stand was launched in the same year on a new model called "The Jubilee Safety Horse" in time for Queen Victoria's Jubilee Celebrations. Curiously, the Jubilee stand was far more popular in the U.S. than it was in Britain. A case, perhaps, of the grass being greener on the other side!

Catering for all ends of the market, G. & J. Lines offered horses in seven different sizes, from the smallest, measuring only 19 inches in height with 38 inch-long rockers to the largest – 45 inches high with rockers over 6½ feet long. In addition, customers were offered a choice of having their horse with "ordinary finish," "extra carved/best finished," "polished rockers/special finish," and "skin-covered," the most expensive. For a little extra, the company would add saddlebags and straps for babies to ride in, or seats attached to the ends of the rockers.

Joseph Lines's sons worked in the business, but at the end of the war the common problem in family businesses of the old resenting the progressive ideas of the young caused a rift, and three of his sons left in 1919 to start their own firm, Lines Bros. Joseph Lines, having bought out his brother George in 1903, continued in business until his death in 1931.

Their progressive ideas brought lasting success to the Lines brothers, although these notions had been the cause of the rift with their father, to whom the thought of such innovations as metal rocking horses must have been anathema. Determined to keep ahead of the competition, they kept up with the times and were one of the few rocking-horse manufacturers to survive both the Depression of the 1930s and the disruption of World War II. They anticipated the threat looming at the end of World War I from metal toys and the new horseless carriages, and their foresight in developing the manufacturing processes involved in producing metal toys paid off.

In the 1920s Lines Bros. toys were sold under the registered trade name "Tri-ang Toys." Many of the rocking horses sold under this banner were obviously intended for the lower end of the market. True to Lines Bros.' policy of keeping up with the times, some of the horses metamorphosed into Mickey Mouse and other popular cartoon characters of the day. It is possible that this move to incorporate the popular end of the market enabled them to weather the trade depression of the 1930s that drove so many other manufacturers out of business.

Their meteoric success was sustained. Lines Bros. became a quoted company only 14 years after it was formed, exporting rocking horses all over the world. It continued for many more years, and, indeed, was still there to supply their top-of-the-range rocking horse to Queen Elizabeth II for Prince Charles in 1950. Although it still produced wooden rocking horses, these were different in style from those of G. & J. Lines, having much shorter necks, and differences in both materials and methods of manufacture distinguish its horses from those of G. & J. Lines.

Although not as prolific as G. & J. Lines or Lines Bros., the firm of F. H. Ayres of London, formed in the 1860s, manufactured a broad selection of beautifully crafted rocking horses in addition to goods for all indoor and outdoor games and sports – the name is to be found on many an old cricket bat and croquet mallet. Ayres supplied horses to prestigious stores such as Harrods and Selfridges. They were mounted on bow rockers, swing stands, spring rockers, and tricycles. A rare collector's item is a rocking horse made by F. H. Ayres, of which only two have been found in Britain. This horse incorporated the features outlined in F. H. Ayres's patent of 1888, which detailed a device he had invented to enable the horse's head to swivel, independent of the body.

Like those of G. & J. Lines, Ayres horses were offered in different grades of finish and in eight sizes. Since the firm exported its line of sporting goods to Australia, it is likely that some Ayres horses found their way there also. In 1940 the stock, goodwill, and trademarks of F. H. Ayres Ltd. were bought by Sykes & Co. Ltd. of Yorkshire, another sporting goods manufacturer which had diversified into rocking horse manufacture.

**LEFT** **The reproduction made from an original found by David and Noreen Kiss, rocking-horse makers in Britain, of the rare F. H. Ayres swivel-head horse. The stand on which the horse is mounted is also an exact replica of the one made by F. H. Ayres. Height 36 inches, length 60 inches. (David and Noreen Kiss, England)**

## AMERICAN MAKERS

The impact of British design on early American hobby horses was tempered by a strong German influence. The latter was the result not only of the high proportion of German immigrants to the U.S. and Canada in the 1800s but, later, the competition between American and German manufacturers.

American rocking-horse manufacturers developed their own style, however, and commercially produced rocking horses, although never as large as the huge rockers found in British nurseries, were more colorful. American carriagebuilding had produced craftsmen skilled in achieving faultless finishes and exquisite decorative ornamentation on vehicles. This expertise was transferred to the embellishment of rocking horses, and a feature of old American horses is the appearance of beautifully executed painting on the square flat deck between the rockers of a type commonly found also on sledges and toboggans. Surviving painting of this kind greatly enhances the value of old horses. Bow rockers, too, were given

special treatment, with fine lines, pinstripes, and scrolls in colors attractive to their young riders – red, green, and yellow with contrasting bands of different colors. Papier-mâché horses were also made in the U.S. and were being sold by the Chicago firm of Montgomery Ward & Co. in the second half of the 19th century.

Although dozens of workshops sprang up between the 1850s and the turn of the century, many were in business for only a short time before either being forced out of business or joining the equally booming craft of carousel-horse manufacture. Merry-go-round horses were an entirely different breed, usually ornately carved and painted with highly colored and lavish designs in the fairground tradition. Charles W. F. Dare of the New York Carousel Manufacturing Company seems also to have made toy hobby horses. These have an innocent quality, with cute, plump faces and mouths that smile in spite of over-tight nosebands. In place of the usual leather saddles, they had wooden saddles, separately carved and mounted onto the horse. A distinctive feature of Dare horses is that they have marbles for eyes,

BELOW **A late 18th-century American horse-head rocker with hand-lining, scrolling, and grapevine motif. (Shelburne Museum, Shelburne, Vermont)**

LEFT **Martha's Vineyard Carousel produced in 1878 by Charles W. F. Dare. The horse is ornately carved with typical glass eyes and smiling face. (*New England Carousel Museum*)**

alternating between swirls and clear glass sulfides containing small animal motifs.

It is possible that the enthusiasm for merry-go-round horses had something to do with the more colorful appearance of American rocking horses. The racy posture of the merry-go-round horses was echoed in the outstretched stance of some rocking horses and could have accounted for the popularity in the U.S. of the underslung Jubilee stand of G. & J. Lines, which made this possible because the belly and not the legs of the horse was attached to the stand.

LEFT **A rare horse by Ernest Kirch of Massachusetts, typical of his style with a long narrow head and detailed carvings of facial features, c.1871. Height 63½ inches, length 123 inches. (*Courtesy The Strong Museum, Rochester, New York*)**

LEFT **A rare horse by Ernest Kirch of Massachusetts typical of his style with a long narrow head and detailed carvings of facial features, c.1871. Height 161cm (63½in), length 312cm (123in). (Courtesy the Strong Museum, Rochester, New York)**

In the 1800s there were rocking-horse makers in at least 12 states, with the highest concentration in Ohio, Pennsylvania, Massachusetts, and New York. In Cincinnati, Ohio, there was a thriving wood-working community, with wood-carving schools and workshops, and, of course, P. J. Marqua of swing stand fame. Pennsylvania benefited from the skill of its strong German community coupled with the fact that rocking horses had been commercially produced there since the 18th century. Massachusetts – the home of the famous Boston Rocker, patented by A. Woodworth III, D. Woodworth, and M. T. Hitchcock in 1859 – boasted Bradford Kingman, the Morton E. Converse Toy Company, the largest in the country, and the famous Whitney Reed Corporation.

The invention of American makers knew no bounds, although many horses were but a variation on a theme. An exception appears in Patricia Mullins's history of moving toy horses in the form of an elegant rocking horse invented by Ernst Kirch of Massachusetts in 1871. The body and rockers of this unusual horse were constructed out of bentwood. Its contemporary appearance may have been ahead of its time, which would account for the fact that few examples are to be found.

In contrast, innovations produced by some of the many New York makers were more commercially successful. Aimed at toddlers, rocking-horse chairs were very popular and were developed in myriad forms and degrees of sophistication. The superb Boston Rocker, its sleigh-like lines providing a perfect canvas for the best of decorative art, was the first to appear.

Benjamin Potter Crandall and his four sons were at the forefront of this particular kind of innovation. Crandall, Sr., originally made baby buggies and perambulators, then added rocking-horse chairs to his range of nursery furniture, having derived the idea from the old board-sided design of early

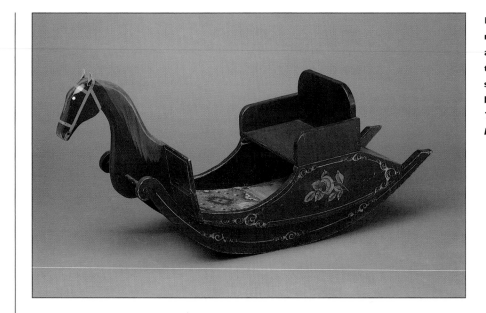

LEFT **A typical horse head rocker with a low slung body and child's seat, c.1900. Note the gold decoration on the sides: panel height 53 inches, length 20 inches. (Courtesy The Strong Museum, Rochester, New York)**

German rocking horses. From this, his son Jesse took the idea a step further and only three months after the Boston Rocker appeared, his patent for the famous "shoofly" rocking chair was granted. His brother, William Edward Crandall, patented a further version of the shoofly in 1870, and their designs were to be adopted by manufacturers all over the world for many years to come. The shoofly served a different market from the Boston Rocker. Cheap and easy to make and involving little or no carving,

ABOVE **Two examples of the shooflies on offer by L. H. Mace & Co. of New York at** the beginning of the 20th century. **(Washington Dolls' House and Toy Museum)**

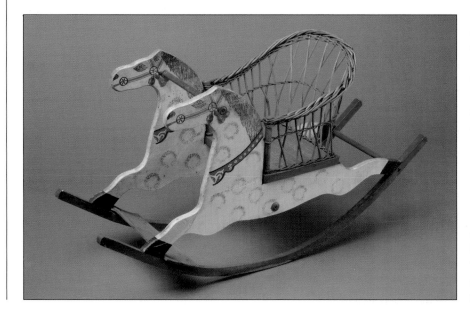

LEFT **A fine example of a shoofly with wicker chair, c.1915. Horse heads and front legs are printed and painted on both sides. Height 53 inches, length 95 inches. (Courtesy The Strong Museum, Rochester, New York)**

ABOVE **Infant Rocker sold by L. H. Mace & Co. of New York in 1907. (Washington Dolls' House and Toy Museum)**

its simple form consisted of two flat cut-out animals mounted on a rocking base.

Over a period of about 60 years, various members of the Crandall family were responsible for many other rocking horse-related inventions, which incorporated just about every conceivable way of emulating the movement of a horse. None of them quite reached the degree of fame as the shoofly, although Jesse Crandall's invention involving a flat coiled spring was moderately successful.

The spring horse, designed and manufactured by Andrew Christian of New York in the 1860s, was another sound invention on which the height could be varied by altering the spring mechanism. Christian later joined with Charles W. F. Dare, who is better known as a manufacturer of merry-go-round horses. Dare also made children's vehicles, rocking horses, velocipedes and baby buggies, among which was the famous "Tally Ho" series of gigs and sulkies, which were made in various types and sizes to suit different ends of the market. Some of these charming vehicles had a flat area beneath the seat which was often painted in a similar style to the decks between bow rockers.

No commentary on American innovations would be complete without mentioning the impeccably elegant convertible chair/rocking horse patented by J. A. Nichols in 1878. This masterpiece of design was an ergonomic delight and could be utilized in three ways – as a high chair, a rocking chair, or a wheeled "carriage" chair. Classed as an item of children's furniture rather than as a toy, this chair was finished in a manner appropriate to furniture, and the richness of the stained and polished item was mirrored in the muted colors of the two horse's heads.

Perhaps the most beautiful American rocking horse surviving from the 19th century was not made by any of the commercial manufacturers of the time. Exquisitely carved, it was made by a British woodcarver named John Bryant who immigrated to San Francisco in 1847. Obviously a carver of high skill, his work was mainly within Grace Cathedral and opulent mansions. He made the horse, which can be seen in the Oakland Museum in California, for his children.

The longest-lasting and most prolific hobby-horse makers were old-established firms, one of which was that of Adolphe Meinecke of Milwaukee. Meinecke was a German immigrant who, although primarily a furniture maker, produced all sorts of rocking horses and rocking chairs from the middle of the century until 1929 when, like many others, his business was ended by the Great Depression.

The Morton E. Converse Toy Company in Massachusetts was also one of the casualties. Another family firm, this time father and son, it became one of the largest toy-making companies in the U.S. in the course of its half-century of trading. Converse rocking horses were produced in both painted and skin-covered finishes. Morton Converse was keen to give his horses realism and, realizing that the mood of real horses can often be gauged by the way they hold their ears, patented an invention with movable ears in 1896. Whether or not the company went into production with this invention is not clear, but none is currently known to exist, so if you come across a rocking horse with moving ears you have a rare item!

Morton Converse's main rival was the Whitney Reed Corporation, also of Massachusetts. Rocking horses from the two companies differed little except that Whitney Reed heads are distinguishable by the two quite deep grooves carved on the muzzle. Perhaps because they also made furniture, or maybe because they had an astonishing choice of horse toys for children, Whitney Reed survived the Depression years. It favored the G. & J. Lines Jubilee stand, and Whitney Reed models, like Converse horses, are recognizable by their raised heads and outstretched legs indicating speed. Horses on bow rockers were also made, and plush- and skin-covered models were, like their British counterparts, made of solid wood rather than stuffed as German horses were. Often the ears are missing on old Converse and Whitney Reed horses, largely because the ears of all the horses were of leather and, like original harnesses, they have not survived.

At the beginning of World War II, Whitney Reed was quick to fill the gap created by the sudden suspension of European imports and brought out a series of new models. Included were the "Center Swing Horse," where the horse straddled a central pillar, leaving the legs free, and a "Spring Frame Swing Horse," with heavy coil springs adjustable to different weights, which was modeled on an earlier European device. The dapples on Whitney Reed horses were more spot-like than those of British horses and covered the whole body of the horse rather than being focused on certain parts.

Although it survived both the Great Depression and World War II, the company ceased trading in the 1950s. Despite a valiant attempt by Herb Green, who had bought the company in the 1930s, to keep up with the latest manufacturing techniques, it was defeated finally by a lack of demand for the steeds of yesteryear from children who opted for modern toys.

LEFT **This 19th-century skin-covered horse by Whitney Reed on long bow rockers is a good example of both German and British influences on American hobby-horse makers. This horse was sold at auction by Skinner Inc. of Boston in 1989 for $4,800. (By permission of Skinner Inc., Boston)**

## CANADIAN MAKERS

One of the most skilled of woodcarvers was the talented Moritz Eduard Lindner, a German immigrant who settled with his family in Berlin (now Kitchener), Ontario. In the 1860s he started in business making baby buggies, sleighs, and toy horses of all kinds. He had a wide repertoire, which included rocking horses, velocipedes, wheeled horses, chaired horses, and all kinds of related novelties as well as life-size horses for store displays. He patented a variation of the German stuffed horses based on a body of stiffened, molded canvas. His enterprise was successful, there being few other makers of toy horses in Canada, and his main competition was from imported horses.

## FRENCH MAKERS

The French preoccupation with cycling led to an innovation that appeared at the beginning of the 19th century. Inspired by the invention of the bicycle, two inventors, Jean Louis Gourdoux of Paris and a M. Courbe, registered patents for horses on tricycles in 1821 and 1822 respectively. The rockers were replaced by wheels, and one of these horses, known in Britain as "Pedestrian Hobby-Horse," was pushed along by the small rider's feet. Such horses were the forerunners of mechanical versions — tricycle horses or velocipedes. These had mechanisms propelling the horses along — early ones being foot treadles and hand cranks. Once the principle of velocipedes had been defined, it was refined and developed by manufacturers all over the world. Although traditional horses on rockers were also made, they were nowhere near as popular in France as these dainty little velocipedes.

The stance most suited to the design of velocipedes had the horse rearing, with its two front legs in the air, and the steering column sometimes

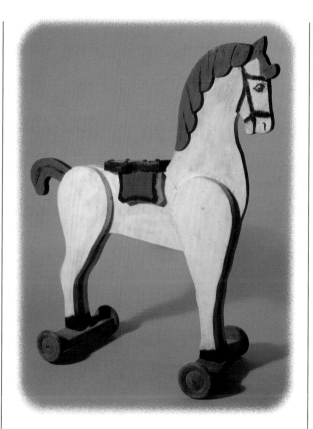

ABOVE **A wooden horse on wheels from the Lille region in France, dated around 1925, painted white with spots, black hooves, and a red mane. Height 27½ inches. (Union Centrale des Arts Décoratifs Musée, Paris, France)**

ABOVE **Advertisement for tricycle horses from the Harrods catalog of 1895. (With thanks to Mohamed Al** **Fayed, Chairman of Harrods Ltd., for permission to use the illustration)**

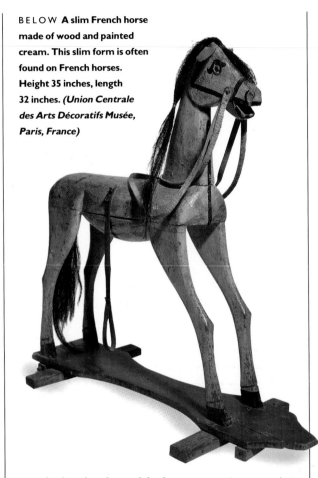

BELOW **A slim French horse made of wood and painted cream. This slim form is often found on French horses. Height 35 inches, length 32 inches. (Union Centrale des Arts Décoratifs Musée, Paris, France)**

attached to the chest of the horse, sometimes passing through a hole in the horse's body, and emerging at the top of the neck. This same stance can be seen on French platform-mounted and rocking horses, with the raised body supported on a cast-iron pole attached to the platform.

The French also used painted papier-mâché for small platform and rocking horses, but the wood and metal construction of their larger horses was distinctively French. The use of metal stemmed from the need to provide a strong base for the steering column on tricycle horses. Heads were cast in molds in two parts, with holes for the eyes and reins, as well as for the handle grips and steering column.

Wrought iron was used for both rockers and the tricycle frame and wheels. Early tricycle horses had wooden wheels with iron tires, but most later models have metal wheels with solid rubber tires. The

wrought ironwork around the chain mechanism on some velocipedes was delicately ornate and typically French in design, as were their slender bodies. The firm of A. Garnier was a major manufacturer of rocking horses and tricycle horses from 1890 until 1922, and their elaborate cast-iron supports make the company's tricycle horses easily recognizable.

Although velocipedes were enormously popular, not only in France but elsewhere, they were accident-prone, and many of their parts were vulnerable to the inevitably robust use. The castings were brittle and liable to crack, the mechanisms wore out, and stresses at points where metal met wood weakened the structure. As a result, few very old velocipedes have survived intact. Those dating from the end of the 19th century will undoubtedly have been repaired at some time. Their charm has not diminished, however, and the designs outlasted early samples. Today, they are still lovingly and faithfully copied by firms specializing in reproductions.

The products of French manufacturers reflected both their own inventions and those developed elsewhere, particularly those of a mechanical nature. As in other countries, calfskin as well as plush fabric was used to cover luxury models. A late

BELOW **A Garnier advertisement from its 1922 catalog. (Union Centrale des Arts Décoratifs Musée, Paris, France)**

entry to the field was the firm of Pintel in Paris which from 1920 until 1963 made a range of plush-covered animals on wheels and rockers that proved to be very popular in France.

The painting on papier-mâché horses made by Clerc & Sons makes them easily recognizable – they have all-over patterns of large brown spots.

Surprisingly, when you think of the sociological turmoil they have undergone, many French rocking-horse firms of the 19th and early 20th centuries have survived to the present day, notable of which are the oldest: Arbre à Jouer, established in 1870, Clairbois, Cornu, and Leon Giraud-Sauveur.

ABOVE *Cheval à pedale* with pedals on the front wheel, made in France c.1920. The head turns with the wheel and pedal movement. The saddle is maroon, and the three wheels red. Height 24½ inches. *(Union Centrale des Arts Décoratifs Musée, Paris, France)*

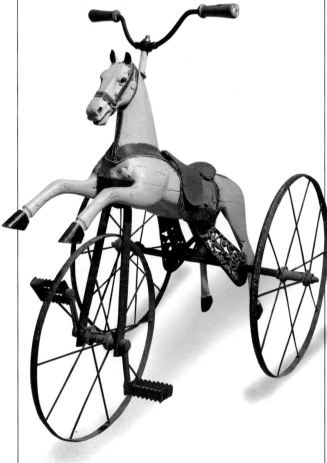

ABOVE **Dainty little French tricycle horse with leather saddle and harness, c.1880. Note the slender, elegant lines of the horse, which is typically French, and was** possibly made by Garnier. Height 33 inches, length 31 inches. *(Union Centrale des Arts Décoratifs Musée, Paris, France)*

ABOVE **A brown velvet horse on a wheeled platform, made in France in 1913. The wooden platform base measures 9×8 inches and the** height of the horse is 30½ inches. *(Union Centrale des Arts Décoratifs Musée, Paris, France)*

## BELGIAN MAKER

The firm of Nazaire Beeusaert of Belgium was a major exporter of wheeled platform and rocking horses. From the late 1800s until 1939, the factory turned out large numbers of painted papier-mâché horses in a range of different sizes. It has to be said that Nazaire Beeusaert horses had a somewhat unsophisticated shape, and, in fact, some of their models bore a distinct resemblance to dogs rather than horses. However, this obviously did not deter the customers, because the company's horses sold in great quantities.

## AUSTRALIAN MAKERS

Life was hard in Australia in the early days after the first settlements at the end of the 1700s, and it was not until late in the 19th century that the first commercial manufacturers of rocking horses appeared, commercial enterprise being inhibited by the vast size of the country. Consequently, most horses would have been homemade.

Patricia Mullins, who herself lives in Australia, studied Australian rocking-horse manufacturers extensively and found two family firms that stand out: Frederick Roebuck, a British expatriate based in Sydney, was one of the first indigenous makers of rocking horses, and Robert Bartlett of Melbourne, a woodworker with a background in furniture-making, was another.

The design and style of Australian horses were, naturally, very similar to those of British horses, which were being imported in quantity at the time.

**ABOVE Small "rocker colt" (original condition) made by F. Roebuck and Sons Pty. Ltd. Sydney, c.1960. A copying lathe, introduced by the firm in the 1930s, was used in the manufacture of this horse. (Patricia Mullins, author *The Rocking Horse*. Photograph: Ray Kinnane)**

**LEFT Rocking horse (original condition) made by Frederick Roebuck, Sydney, c.1910. The methods of construction and finishing follow the English style. (Patricia Mullins, author *The Rocking Horse*. Photograph: Ray Kinnane)**

RIGHT **Rocking and pull-
along horses made by John
Bartlett, Melbourne, 1960–
1970. The rocking horses are
handmade and finished, and
bear little difference from
those produced by the
Bartlett firm in the early 20th
century. (Patricia Mullins,
author *The Rocking Horse*.
Photograph: Ray Kinnane)**

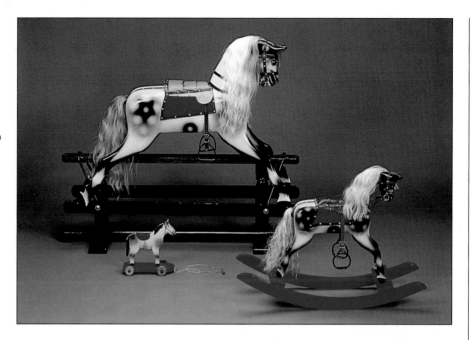

Roebuck's horses bore a marked resemblance to those of Ayres, and it is likely that Roebuck had been familiar with the design before his arrival in Australia in the 1880s. His horses can be distinguished from those of Bartlett by their well-shaped fetlocks and hooves.

Robert Bartlett modeled his horses on those of G. & J. Lines, but the feature that makes some Bartlett models most readily identifiable is the dappling, which has a distinctive diamond pattern. Another is that his horses never had gesso on the lower legs or on the belly.

Another Australian maker was Lou Peets, a blacksmith who had come from England in the early 1900s and was in business making rocking horses for 50 years. Peets's horses are probably the easiest of all to identify because of his unusual and somewhat stylized method of dappling.

Australian makers came into their own at the onset of World War I when the traffic in imported goods ceased, and the groundwork was laid to prepare them for the boom in the industry at the end of the war. Roebuck and Bartlett dominated the market and divided the territory between them.

The cheap and cheerful shoofly, while not as esthetically pleasing as the larger, more graceful rocking horses, was very popular in Australia and was manufactured in great quantity.

## DEPRESSION AND DECLINE

Elsewhere, the rocking horse industry never really recovered from the effects of the Great Depression of the 1930s, sandwiched as it was between two world wars. Rocking-horse manufacturers tried to keep up with the trend by adapting their designs and cutting manufacturing costs, but they were fighting a losing battle. The Depression sounded the death knell, and even previously successful and long-established businesses such as Converse in the U.S. and F. H. Ayres in Britain went out of business soon after.

The introduction of metal for toy-making and the replacement of the horse by the automobile as a mode of transportation, coupled with the decreasing size of new houses, accelerated the decline. Outsold by mass-produced toys that mirrored contemporary reality more accurately, rocking horses were relegated to dusty attics.

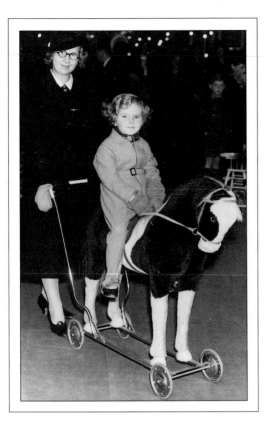

# POST-WAR ROCKING HORSES

## CHAPTER 3

During the two world wars, many toy factories in countries at war, if not actually ceasing operation, were compelled to turn over production to essential goods and munitions. After each war there came a mini-boom in the rocking-horse industry, but both were short-lived.

Amid the euphoria and optimistic spirit of the years after World War II, people were at last able to think about non-essentials. Factories slowly wound back into production, and in the 1950s, for a while, it looked as if the rocking-horse industry would recover. However, the demand was soon overtaken by the new generation of "tin toys," which almost completely ousted traditional rocking horses. Suitable for mass-production and cheaper to make, these new toys took myriad forms. The age of throwaway toys had arrived.

LEFT **Fabric-covered horses take precedence at a Toy Fair in London, England in 1936.** *(Fox Photos Ltd., London)*

BELOW **Reproduction of one of the "Swallow Toys" produced by G. Woodrow & Co. Ltd. of London, England. Some similarities to G. & J. Lines products – dappling and hoof shape – are evident, probably because G. Woodrow worked with G. & J. Lines for over 20 years.** *(Stevenson Brothers, Kent, England)*

## THE ROCKING HORSE WINNER

As if two world wars and a major depression weren't enough, in Britain the rocking horse industry was dealt another blow, this time from a completely unexpected quarter. Throughout the drab war years, movies had played an important part in people's lives. Television had not yet arrived, and the film industry was thriving. In 1949 the Rank Organisation made a film starring John Mills called *The Rocking Horse Winner* by D. H. Lawrence. The story was centered around a rocking horse on whose back a small boy could predict the winners of horse races. Predictably, the boy's ability was exploited, and the film depicted the abuse of the boy rather horribly. The rocking horse in the film was portrayed as a malevolent object, and a whole generation of children and parents was alienated. It was to be another 30 years before the industry really recovered. The few established firms that pulled through this troubled time were those that diversified their range to incorporate the new generation of toys or that had other successful product lines.

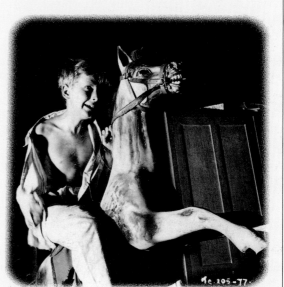

**ABOVE** Scene from *The Rocking Horse Winner* made by Rank Films in 1949. *(British Film Institute)*

## END OF AN ERA

European rocking-horse manufacturers were also trying to pick up the pieces after World War II. Despite the devastation and trauma of military occupation, French makers withstood the onslaught of plastic, metal, and modernity better than others. The reason for this could have been that, although it was occupied territory, factories were not commandeered for the production of munitions as they were in Britain and Germany. N. Clerc et Fils, today part of the Superjouet group, was still making rocking horses in 1940.

Rocking-horse makers in Australia fared better than most; after the end of World War II, there was a boom in the demand for rocking horses there. Frederick Roebuck and his son Norman stepped in to supply it, and for a while business was great; Roebuck turned out thousands of wooden horses during the years immediately after the war and had

**BELOW** Pull-along horse with a paint and flocked finish. It is mounted on a pink-painted wooden wheeled base. Made in France around 1958. Height 23 inches. *(Union Centrale des Arts Décoratifs Musée, Paris, France)*

mechanized some of its manufacturing processes in the 1930s. For some time it had been supplying Cyclops Toys with machine-made wooden components for its toys as a lucrative sideline. However, when Cyclops Toys was taken over by Lines Bros. in the 1950s and renamed Cyclops Lines, the firm's connection with Roebuck petered out. Cyclops Lines made metal and plastic rocking horses to the Lines Tri-ang designs and this, together with competition from cheap imported horses made of metal and plastic, affected Roebuck adversely.

During the next decade, Roebuck's range was reduced to one size of horse only, with a body length of 22 inches, which helped to streamline production. Over the next 20 years, the firm fought back by cutting the quality of its raw materials and trimming manufacturing costs in an attempt to remain competitive. Plastic harnesses replaced leather, cheap pine imported from New Zealand replaced the expensive Oregon pine imported from North America, and some of the carving was now done by machines.

Eventually even cost-cutting exercises were not enough. Cheap Asian toy imports dealt Roebuck a fatal blow when, in the 1970s, import tariffs on toys were removed. The Roebucks retired, but the horses they made did not. Because of the company's high output following World War II, the most commonly found rocking horses in Australia today are theirs, having outlived their plastic and metal rivals.

Lines Bros., with worldwide outlets, was in a good position in the post-war period. Always at the forefront of development, the company had expanded its range far beyond the rocking horses on which the business had been founded, the

ABOVE **A Paterson Edwards horse is still favorite at the 1948 Toy Fair in London.** *(Fox Photos Ltd., London)*

descendants of which were now a very minor part of the Lines Bros. empire of Tri-ang Toys. By the 1950s Lines Bros. rocking horses were pale shadows of the magnificent wooden steeds of yesteryear. The beautifully carved heads had been replaced by molded rubber versions mounted on tubular steel rockers. Twenty years later, even these had been superseded by molded plastic horses.

The famous Lines Bros. formula for success which had served the company so well for so long ultimately failed, however, and the firm suffered an unmerited and ignominious end when it went into liquidation in 1972, leaving J. Collinson & Sons to carry the baton of traditional wooden rocking-horse manufacture in Britain into the future.

The same economic climate that was responsible for the end of Lines Bros. caused the demise of another line of metal rocking horses. With an established manufacturing base in iron and steel products, the firm of D. Sebel & Co. Ltd. of Kent, England, had been successfully selling the brand Mobo Toys for 30 years. The "Mobo Bronco," probably the best-remembered of metal rocking

LEFT **One of D. Sebel's "New Mobo Rocking Horses" produced in the early 1950s. Note the jointed legs. The metal rockers were added to this model in 1952.** *(Stevenson Brothers, Kent, England)*

LEFT **A Baby Carriages Ltd. horse unrestored. Note the painted eye typical of the firm's style.**

horses, introduced yet another way of moving a toy horse around a room. Pressure on the stirrups activated a spring mechanism inside the horse that moved the legs, which had wheels in the feet.

Mobo horses, mass-produced and thus cheaper to make, gave Sebel a virtual monopoly of the British market throughout the 1950s and 1960s. The horses came in a variety of forms in addition to the original version with jointed legs. Molded as they were in solid form, they had obviously been derived from previous design concepts. They were sometimes mounted on tubular metal rockers and stands with springs, at the front of go-karts with pedals, and even the humble Bristol toy was represented in the form of a tiny push-along Mobo horse.

Lacking as they did the warmth of real wood and the individuality of a carved horse, it is hard to imagine a child forming the same fond, personal relationship with them as was possible with traditional wooden rocking horses – the magic was missing. Eventually Sebel, too, ceased production in

the 1970s, probably because of a combination of the missing magic and the plethora of plastic toys invading the toy marketplace.

## THE SURVIVORS

Rocking horses had always been regarded not only as toys, but also as a form of children's furniture, and they were often made as a secondary line by baby-buggy manufacturers. Because of the strength of their other business, such companies were able to continue to make rocking horses, albeit for a reduced market. Like the homes that housed them, rocking horses themselves became smaller. However, they were produced in quantity by three firms better known for their baby buggies – Wilson & Son Ltd. of Leeds, better known for its Silver Cross buggies, Baby Carriages Ltd. of Liverpool, and Paterson Edwards, which made Leeway buggies. Horses from these firms are familiar visitors to today's restorers' workshops, suggesting that they

RIGHT **A Paterson Edwards horse unrestored, mounted on a safety stand.**

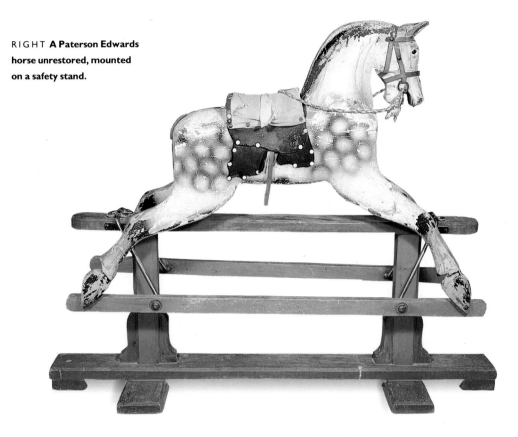

must have been manufactured in some numbers. Margaret Fawdry of Pollock's Toy Museum in London reports in her book *English Rocking Horses* that one of Paterson Edwards's employees, George Brown, said at his retirement in 1966 that in 46 years' service with the company he had made about 35,000 horses – about 800 each year since 1920!

One of the most popular plush-covered rocking horses of all time, Merrythought's successful "Pablo Donkey," has an unusual history. The grandfather of

## STEIFF

A more drastic metamorphosis can be seen in the rocking horses of the German firm of Steiff, whose lineage goes back to the late 19th century. Throughout the decades after World War II, the design of its plush horses gradually moved away from the traditional, well-shaped German style, which closely resembled skin-covered horses, to assume a more toy-like, chubby, cuddly appearance. Steiff is another firm whose line was diverse enough to survive the ravages of political, economic, and sociological trauma, and the plush-covered rocking horse it produces today has supported the breed alone since 1982. Because of the continuity of Steiff rocking horses, they offer collectors an opportunity to aim for an unbroken strand of historical record, which makes the company's rocking horses fascinating to collect.

ABOVE **Margarete Steiff horse with the later chubby shape.**

Oliver Holmes, the present owner, had a spinning mill and a weaving mill in the north of England and, looking for an allied operation that would support them, he started a factory in 1930 to manufacture stuffed toys. This undertaking was successful in providing the support he needed for his spinning and weaving mills, but was not particularly profitable in itself. In 1950 his son, who had joined the family business, designed and developed the now-famous Pablo Donkey, which was to become an evergreen favorite, right up to the present day. The Pablo Donkey has meandered happily through the years, paying only mild homage to changing fashion. Not until 1991 was there any major change when, 100 years after the first swing stand was invented, the Pablo Donkey at last joined the other swingers of the rocking-horse clan.

In the U.S. the rocking-horse industry took almost half a century to recover from the effects of the Depression, and American-manufactured horses found today tend, therefore, to be either very old or very new. The demise of this huge section of the toy

ABOVE **A 1962 push-along version of the fabric-covered Pablo Donkey from Merrythought Ltd., with chrome handles, footrests,** **and rubber-rimmed tires. Height 39 inches, length 42 inches. (Courtesy of Oliver Holmes, Merrythought Ltd., England)**

ABOVE **Today's version of the Pablo Donkey is little changed, even to the fringed "Mexican" saddle blanket. The metal rockers have been replaced by elegant wooden shallow bows and a Marqua-** **style safety stand. He seems, however, to have shrunk to 30 inches. The little push-along version has also changed little. (Courtesy of Oliver Holmes, Merrythought Ltd., England)**

industry was a sad fate for a country that had made such a spectacular contribution. However, America's loss is the collector's gain because horses by American makers are even more sought-after collectors' pieces; even reproductions are scarce.

Despite the body blows dealt to this graceful relic of bygone days, the rocking horse industry from the 1950s on, although drastically contracted by the disappearance of the majority of old-established traditional manufacturers, was kept alive by a few stalwarts. In the 1980s, perhaps as a reaction to the diminished values and wasteful lifestyle of the throwaway television age, people responded to a nostalgic yearning for the stability and endurance of bygone things and a new breed of makers emerged to restore something of its former popularity to the venerable and esteemed rocking horse.

# MODERN ROCKING HORSE MAKERS

CHAPTER 4

Although by the 1960s the rocking-horse industry was down, it was not quite out. In Britain the faint stirrings of renewed interest in traditional toys in the late 1970s grew to blossom into a full-scale renaissance of the industry in the booming 1980s. The present-day market is segmented into three different types of rocking horse: those built in the traditional manner and made of wood; fiberglass and plastic horses; and fluffy, plush-covered versions.

One of the first to join the old-established firms in the field in the 1970s was Relko, which later expanded its operation to New Zealand. Constructed of laminated wood, Relko horses are easily distinguished by the swirling patterns of the layers of wood.

Several small workshops making traditional rocking horses were set up in Britain at about the same time, including that of Margaret Spencer, a lifelong rocking-horse enthusiast, in Somerset, and, in the north of England, John and Dorothy Woods. It is possible that the Woods are the only British manufacturers who are currently making skin-covered horses. There are two types: those carved in wood and covered in skin, and those with a wooden head and legs with a body filled with wood shavings or straw. The skins are generally fitted over a wooden frame and covered in calfskin, with only the very largest horses being covered in horse skin. The Woods' expertise is not confined to skin-covered horses, however, and they make a range of over 20 different types of rocking horses, from the traditional dapple gray to those with a natural varnished finish. They also restore all types of horses: traditional wooden dapple grays, skin-covered horses, plush-covered horses and those made of fiberglass, pressed steel, and even plastic.

ABOVE **A large bow rocker made by John and Dorothy Woods of England. Carved in mahogany with natural finish. Approx. height 48 inches, length 84 inches.**

LEFT An early Stevenson Brothers horse, dating from 1983, which was commissioned for a customer to stand beside an indoor swimming pool. The horse, saddle, and mane are carved out of solid pitch pine, which makes it very heavy.

By the beginning of the 1980s, workshops were springing up all over England and Wales, and there are almost as many small makers now as there were in the boom days of the 19th century. Most of those who make rocking horses in the traditional style also do restoration work on old horses and, particularly at the top end of the market, some makers specialize in reproductions.

Stevenson Brothers of Kent, England, is among the major manufacturers of traditional wooden rocking horses today in Britain. In a Kent workshop the firm carries on a family tradition begun by the Stevensons' Suffolk uncle, James Bosworthick, an old-fashioned craftsman, who had been making hand-carved traditional rocking horses for many years. However, the company's designs are quite different from those of Bosworthick.

Another of today's English rocking horse makers is Anthony Dew who started making rocking horses at the end of the 1970s. He now runs The Rocking Horse Shop in Yorkshire, England with his wife, Pat, where they make and restore rocking horses, as well as supplying a wide range of plans and accessories for rocking horse makers and restorers.

Since the firm's inception in 1982, Stevenson Brothers has specialized in faithful reproductions of beautiful old traditional rocking horses. So successful have these been that, at a trade fair in London, antique experts were unable to tell the difference between an original and a Stevenson Brothers reproduction! Fortunately, the firm has always marked the stand-bases and rockers of its horses with a brass plaque engraved with the name

ABOVE Reproduction of a German "Zoo" horse, first produced c.1923.

**ABOVE A large pinto-painted horse on a safety stand, by Stevenson** **Brothers, commissioned by an American client.**

of the firm, the year of manufacture, and the number of the horse so that collectors can identify them. Like those other famous English brothers, the Lines, the Stevensons export their horses all over the world.

The Stevensons' reputation for being able to produce whatever the customer wants has resulted in the creation of some charming and unusual horses, including a display horse hand-carved by Tony Stevenson, which can be seen in Harrods of London. This horse bears more than a passing resemblance to those produced by the skilled carver Moritz Lindner of Ontario in the 1890s.

Another special request could possibly have been to prevent sibling strife. Although the size of families in most countries has reduced to two or three children, this is not always the case. In 1989 Stevenson Brothers built a full-sized merry-go-round with 12 fully carved and painted horses and two carriages for the many children of the Sultan of Brunei.

Tony Stevenson has been responsible for training some of Britain's best carvers, including David Kiss, who began his rocking-horse career with Stevenson Brothers in the 1980s. Together with his wife, Noreen, an artist, expert restorer, and dedicated rocking-horse aficionado, he operates The Rocking Horse Workshop in Shropshire. Kiss's first love was the automobile, and he has restored many beautiful

**LEFT One of a range of hand-carved wooden rocking horses made by Anthony Dew of The Rocking Horse Shop, Yorkshire, England. The horse measures 38in to the top of the saddle and the overall length of the stand is 60in.**

LEFT **This "Ashfield" mahogany horse by David and Noreen Kiss combines the grace of Victorian styling with the warmth and richness of natural timber in this lovely, bow-mounted rocking horse.**

RIGHT **This selection of rocking horses in light and dark oak from the Stevenson Brothers stable illustrates the beauty and luster of natural finishes. Note the position of the brass plaque on the stand base.**

old cars to perfection. He has, however, resisted the temptation to use his skill in attaining perfect glossy finishes, preferring the traditional finish of the old craftsmen, with a preference for the style of F. H. Ayres.

The Kisses were fortunate enough to find one of the very rare examples of the F. H. Ayres's swivel-headed horse patented in 1887, and they specialize

ABOVE **A rocking horse in polished utile made in 1990 by Robert Mullis of Wiltshire, England, who makes new horses in the traditional manner. The identification plate on Mullis horses is on the stand top at the front. Height 34 inches.**

in producing reproductions of this horse, faithful even to the design of the pillar and brackets (see photograph on page 63). Horses at the top end of the line are marked with a letter D carved under the belly, while a leaflet of interest to future generations is placed in the cavity of every horse during construction. How helpful such steps would have been to collectors if makers of olden days had had such foresight!

In addition to making reproductions of horses that are almost indistinguishable from their real antique brethren, both the Stevensons and the Kisses also make new horses in their own designs.

Not all modern British makers specialize in reproductions; some, such as Robert Mullis of Wiltshire, make only new horses, but in the traditional manner. Like many before him, Robert Mullis came into rocking-horse making from a background of wagon-body building and carpentry with an old firm of machinery contractors.

The Lines Bros. trademark lives on in its successors, Sharna-Tri-ang Ltd, which now produces metal and fabric rocking horses in Manchester, England, while the steeds of J. Collinson & Sons rock on as they have done for more than a century and a half.

A few French entrepreneurs who joined the ranks of rocking-horse manufacturers in the 1950s have been long-lived. One is the firm of Blanchet, founded in 1953 and still making plush-covered horses on rockers and wheels. Another, Guy Grelety, manufactures painted wooden cut-out horses as well as more sophisticated plush-covered models.

The giant Superjouet group, which includes the old-established firms of Clairbois and Favre in Moirans-en-Montagne, is still producing plush-covered horses on metal and wooden wheels and rockers. Also operating in Moirans-en-Montagne is the firm of Villet Frères, which has been making rocking horses since 1939 under the trademark of "Vilac." Horses in the current line are called Stormy and are made of painted or lacquered wood.

The current popularity of traditional rocking horses is not an assurance of demand, as was discovered by the French firm Les Jouets Taiga, which, at the beginning of the 1980s, produced large, modern carved horses, with real horsehair manes and mounted on safety rockers. The company was unable to find a large enough market, so

production ceased – bad news for Les Jouets Taiga, but good news for collectors, as these luxury horses could easily become the sought-after rarities of the future.

Throughout the centuries the more stylish rocking horses have tended to be made by woodcarvers or sculptors. Remy Serret, a contemporary rocking-horse maker, is a sculptor who produces elegantly carved wooden horses on bow rockers. Apart from the obvious artistry involved in their carving, his horses are distinguishable from modern British horses by the grip handles on each side of the neck.

The horses of another current maker, La Sauterelle, also have grip handles on each side of the neck. The firm's popular rocking animals are made from colored woods, and the range includes rocking grasshoppers and insects as well as horses.

Today two manufacturers lead the field in Australia – Heirloom Rocking Horses in New South Wales and Christopher Woolcock in Tasmania.

ABOVE **A rocking horse and a rocking donkey from the current Steiff range.**

In Germany, horses built on frames and covered with skin, plush, burlap, or velvet are still being made in small workshops and by large manufacturers, such as the firm of Biggi, whose trademark appears internationally. The old-established firms of Merrythought and Steiff still dominate the plush-covered market in Europe, and their horses are to be found in most countries as both companies have thriving export businesses.

The huge North American marketplace is the target of rocking-horse exporters from other countries, but, as in Britain, small workshops are springing up. The Rocking Horse Gallery in Virginia is the focal point of a group of aspiring rocking-horse makers. Run by David and Faylee Hydorn, the gallery exhibits and sells locally made horses.

ABOVE **Hand-carved, limited-edition horse in pinewood, whitewashed and antiqued by Bob and Gail** **Clifford and sold by the Rocking Horse Gallery in Virginia.**

In Nevada, Red Walsh transferred his skill in decorating his pizza parlor in Bavarian and Gay Nineties style to his "Rock-o Kritters." Red caught the carving bug when his wife Norma asked him if he could make a teeter-totter (seesaw) for their grandchildren out of a beautiful piece of slab oak given to them by a neighboring storekeeper. From the horses' heads with handles he built onto the seats of the seesaw, he went on to build rocking horses, then rocking animals of all kinds and even merry-go-round horses. Norma makes quality reproduction dolls, and together they sell their work at the Virginia Junction Doll and Toy Shoppe in Carson City, Nevada.

The attraction of collecting rocking horses from small workshops is that their horses are usually made by people with a real feeling for these magical toys from the past. The standards of creativity and workmanship are frequently high and well worth investigating. Who knows, your grandchildren might thank you for buying these antiques of the future!

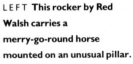

LEFT **This rocker by Red Walsh carries a merry-go-round horse mounted on an unusual pillar.**

# TRACING THE BLOODLINE

CHAPTER 5

A common problem facing the collector is to determine whether the rocking horse is an old one, a reproduction, or a fake. The makers of most modern-day reproductions pursue their craft out of an admiration for craftsmen of old and a desire to continue fine traditional designs. Customers like their reproduction horse to look like an original, and so the finish on a horse is often "distressed" to give it the appearance of being really old. On the whole, reproductionists make no secret of the fact that their horses are copies, but not all traders are so scrupulous. The unwary (and sometimes the not-so-unwary) can be fooled by new horses deliberately distressed and passed off as antiques. It is not uncommon, for instance, for restorers to be presented with a reproduction horse distressed to the point where the new owners thought it was in need of repair!

Many of the finest rocking horses have been made by the parents and grandparents of their first riders who put a great deal of love into their handiwork. Rocking horses tend to become part of the family, so the history of the horse also encompasses that of the family, and this is all part of the fascination of tracing a horse's pedigree. Sadly, unless the horse is a family heirloom, this is not always possible, and it would be presumptuous to say that an old rocking horse is of less merit because we cannot pinpoint its exact history.

Commercial makers, on the other hand, left their mark on their rocking horses – if not an actual trade or brand mark, then perhaps a distinctive design, shape, or carving style by which their work can be identified. Some horses can be easily distinguished by their looks alone – for instance, those of J. Collinson & Sons of England are made to a design that has remained unchanged since the 19th

ABOVE **The head of a Lines Bros. horse – note the short neck which distinguishes Lines Bros. models from** G. & J. Lines horses. *(Stevenson Brothers, Kent, England)*

LEFT **Various pillars by Ayres show the different woods and carving styles typical of the company.**

century. There is also no mistaking the elegant lines of Ayres and Lines horses, although they have been much imitated.

Wood carving is an art form and it is inevitable that each maker develops his own distinctive style. Consequently, experts can often precisely identify a horse's maker. Clues can be found in the differences in carving style of heads and bodies, from stand pillars, gliders, hooves, and bow rockers, and, if they have survived the rigors of time, from manes, tails, and harnesses. The best way to make yourself familiar with the varied styles of different makers is to seek out and examine as many old specimens as possible. The guidelines in this chapter, although they will help you to trace the bloodline of your horse, do not presume to be comprehensive, but it is hoped that they will give you an idea of what to look for.

Don't forget that many old horses will have been repaired, sometimes by replacing original pieces, sometimes using more up-to-date materials. In general, the only parts of an old rocking horse you can be absolutely sure are original are fixed wooden and metal parts. Harnesses and movable non-durable parts are not always reliable guides, as they may have been replaced.

Patents, trademarks, and plaques with makers' names make your quest easier. Unfortunately, some makers never put a mark on their horses. The reasons for this could have been that they were modest or didn't think it was important, or even that they were not sufficiently proud of their work to put their names to it! In many instances, however, the reason was simply that the horses were sold through retail outlets, and the name appearing on the horses was that of the retailer rather than the maker.

## LINES BROS PLATES

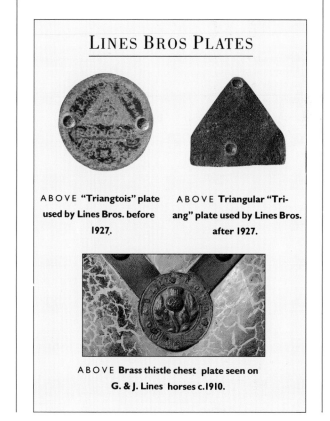

ABOVE **"Triangtois" plate used by Lines Bros. before 1927.**

ABOVE **Triangular "Tri-ang" plate used by Lines Bros. after 1927.**

ABOVE **Brass thistle chest plate seen on G. & J. Lines horses c.1910.**

## CATALOGS

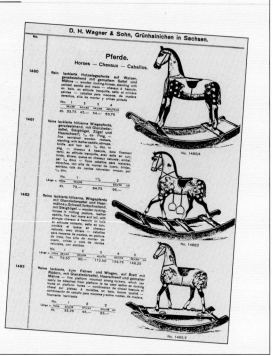

Some larger retailers, for instance Harrods of London and L. H. Mace & Co. of New York, produced illustrated catalogs of toys. While they are useful if you want to find out the date of manufacture of a horse, they often do not mention the actual maker. Some manufacturers themselves, especially those that exported, produced catalogs of their rocking horses. These old catalogs are an invaluable source of information for the serious collector and can sometimes be discovered at antique book fairs or in secondhand book shops. They may be the catalogs of retailers, general toy manufacturers, manufacturers specializing in horse toys, or they could even be from cabinetmakers or baby buggy builders, many of which made rocking horses as ancillary products to their main lines. In recent years reproductions of some German toy catalogs have been published in book form (see Bibliography).

RIGHT **A page from a German toy catalog of D. H. Wagner & Son, c.1905.**

ABOVE **Colorful merry-go-round horse on a safety stand with ornate** carving and carved mane. (*King's Lynn Museum, Norfolk, England*)

You might come across a merry-go-round horse which has been converted into a rocking horse. One such horse, now in the Lynn Museum in King's Lynn, Norfolk, England, has an interesting background. It is believed to have been carved in the 1860s or 1870s for the children of the Savage family who were major manufacturers of merry-go-rounds, and it is obviously adapted from one of their own carousel horses. Carousel conversions are instantly recognizable by the flamboyant carving style, and the saddle and mane were always carved. Be careful with carved saddles, though, because cheap modern imports have this feature, too.

Some, although not many, merry-go-round manufacturers also made rocking horses. One of these was Charles John Spooner of Burton-on-Trent, Staffordshire, England, who made carvings for wagons and showfronts as well as carved panels and animals. He also, however, manufactured two types of rocking horse and two types of push-along toy horses with crudely dappled bodies and manes and tails made of hair. Although the faces of these toy mounts resembled those of Spooner's fairground horses, the rocking and toy horses are far less ornate than their carousel brothers.

LEFT **An imported and badly made horse from the Philippines.**

Merry-go-round horses had to be light enough to be easily handled when the carousel was dismantled to move to another site. Should you encounter an old horse without rockers in a junk shop, if it has thin, flat rear legs and a bowed head it is likely to be a rocker. If it is a merry-go-round horse, there might be traces of a hole for the pole on the top of the animal, but not always because some carousel horses rested on floor mountings.

In some pre-1914 horses, you might find holes under the saddle on each side. These were for side saddle pommels, and the reason there are two is so that girls could change sides from time to time to avoid curvature of the spine.

The kind of materials and finish from which a rocking horse is constructed can give clues as to its pedigree, although they do not provide positive proof, as export trade created a good deal of cross-fertilization. Most makers offered a selection of finishes. G. & J. Lines had three: "Ordinary" (one coat of varnish), "Best" (two coats), and "Special" (extra carved with polished rockers).

Other hints can help; for instance, the shape of the nails used – square-headed nails indicate old age. Restorers of horses often find quite surprising clues inside the body cavity of an old horse – coins, letters, or bits of old newspaper were pushed through the tail hole by previous small owners!

## MATERIALS

The majority of old padded and skin-covered horses originate in Germany. British and American horses of this kind are much rarer, as they usually had the skin tacked or sewn straight onto the solid wooden body and were, therefore, much more expensive than their German counterparts. There were such vast quantities of skin-covered horses turned out that you have to look for additional pointers to identify the manufacturers.

Whitney Reed in the U.S. produced a line of plush-covered horses after the outbreak of World War I when German imports ceased, hoping to cash in on the market. These were made in the British style, plush covering on a wooden body.

Fabric-covered models with soft stuffing suggest the firms of Margarete Steiff in Germany and Merrythought in Britain. Later models from these two companies can look very similar at first glance, having a chunky shape covered in fur fabric. The deciding factor is in the bow rockers: Steiff models originally had wood rockers, changing to metal in the 1970s. The bow rockers on Steiff horses are much shallower, without scroll ends, and the hooves are mounted on a hollow, square platform. Merrythought horses, on the other hand, have moved on from their original "Elvis Presley" type shiny chrome rockers to wooden bows and safety stands. Up until the late 1950s, Steiff horses have a well-shaped appearance, while later models are rounder and stockier. As for earlier models, Margarete Steiff patented a "noiseless rocker" in 1898 with a covering of soft material, and these were manufactured for some 20 years.

Painted papier-mâché was adopted as a medium by many European makers in the 19th and 20th centuries as an alternative to expensive wood and skin covering. It was used extensively, particularly in Germany and France. Evidence of the origins of papier-mâché horses is best gleaned from the painted decorations, which usually reveal national characteristics. Those from alpine areas, for instance, often bear traditional ornamentation of spring flowers, and the colors, too, can identify a particular area.

Early French makers used a variety of materials in conjunction with each other. Some horses had a combination of papier-mâché or wood and metal in their manufacture; a cast metal head was attached to the body of the horse, which was either wood or papier-mâché and mounted on rather elegant, slender metal rockers. The shape of the head and body of these French horses is dainty and delicate, and quite unmistakable.

RIGHT **A papier-mâché horse pull-along toy, maker unknown. This little horse is only 11 inches high.** *(Abby Aldridge Folk Art Center, Virginia)*

## FIBERGLASS HORSES

Fiberglass has been used in the manufacture of rocking horses since the early 1970s – mainly the spring-coil horses made by a firm called Ragamuffin Toys Ltd. of Guernsey in the Channel Islands. Ragamuffin produced about 200 horses before it stopped making them in 1981. Most of them were sold in Britain, and one is in the Bethnal Green Museum in London. Haddon Rocking Horses of Britain currently produces a line of four different sizes of fiberglass rocking horse designed in the traditional style. Fiberglass is an ideal material for horses and will withstand exposure to the elements. It is used extensively for modern coin-in-the-slot mechanized rocking toys in shopping complexes.

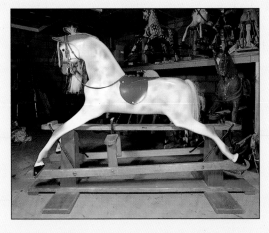

ABOVE **A Haddon rocking horse made of fiberglass.**

## DAPPLING

Gesso began to be used around 1750, but the ever-popular dapple grays did not appear until around 1840. Dappling provides an excellent guide to individual makers – the dappling on an Ayres horse, for instance, is quite distinct, with small, delicate, dapple spots applied by hand. By the 20th century, most horses had only small patches of dapple on each side of the rump, around the belly, above the forelegs, and on each side of the neck.

Firms experimented with different techniques for dappling, and it is not unusual to find several different types of dapple from one manufacturer. For instance, Patricia Mullins, whose early interest in rocking horses was fostered by Jack Bartlett, the son of Australian manufacturer R. J. Bartlett, reports that the latter's horses exhibit three distinct types of dapple. The early horses, dating from 1913 to 1924, were hand-dappled; between 1924 and 1926 Bartlett experimented (unsatisfactorily) with a method of stenciling over round pasted-on spots with an airbrush; after 1926 Bartlett horses were airbrushed freehand, and the dapple on the shoulders and hips of the horse formed a star-like pattern which is quite unmistakable.

## MOUNTING

British 19th-century bow-rocker horses were the largest toys ever made, and those with wicker or metal chairs at each end of the rockers could be up to 8 feet long. The shape of the rockers can provide clues – for example, pre- and early 1870s British and American horses are on deep, boat-shaped rockers. On small horses destined for younger children, the bows were shallower to prevent them from capsizing. These were often painted dark green and sometimes gessoed. The end spacer bars are made of turned wood, and there is a platform in the middle of the rockers (which were made in two halves). This platform was made of strips of softwood about 3 inches wide, which overlapped the rocker sides by about 1 inch. An original platform should show wear marks. If you look underneath the platform, there should be a square box shape upon which the platform rests. The underside was never painted. Any decorative painting on the platform might provide a clue to the country of origin. Painted platforms on 19th-century American horses, echoed the style used by coach and wagon builders.

ABOVE **Turned spacer bars at the bow ends of a G. & J. Lines horse, c.1890–1905.** *(Stevenson Brothers, Kent, England)*

ABOVE **Turned bow end spacers from an F. H. Ayres** horse. *(Stevenson Brothers, Kent, England)*

ABOVE **Bow platform on an F. H. Ayres horse c.1880. Note the green paint and the** scallop marking on the end of the boards. *(Stevenson Brothers, Kent, England)*

ABOVE **Papier-mâché horses could be quite large – this one on a wheeled platform over bow rockers** which was made in Germany c.1850 is 29 inches high and 30 inches long. *(Vogelsang Collection, Germany)*

Typically, German, Scandinavian, and French rocking horses of the 19th and early 20th centuries are smaller than their British counterparts. The bow rockers on these horses are not as deeply curved as British and American examples. Many German horses stand directly on wheeled platforms mounted onto bows, but where there is only a bow rocker, the horse stands on crossbars stretching between the bows, with no mounting platform. Some German horses with a walking stance have four boards, one for each leg.

The finish and ornamentation on bow rockers can usually indicate the nationality of a horse. American

**Fine stenciling on old American infant rocker.**

Turned bow rocker on American horse made in the European style.

bows tend to be distinctive for the exquisitely fine linework and scrolling on the rockers, and they are usually painted in brighter colors than their European counterparts.

Tricycle horses, although originally invented by French toymakers, were copied by makers in other countries, and variations were made in the method of propulsion. A good way of identifying an old tricycle horse is to study the many patents registered in America and Britain. Very early wheeled horses had wooden wheels with iron tires, while later ones had metal wheels with solid rubber tires. Some very basic ones were manufactured on wheeled platforms that were pushed along by the feet.

Horses on bow rockers with a wheeled attachment to convert to pull-along are likely to be German, as they were manufactured in great quantity and were often skin-covered.

Rocking horses mounted on swing stands date from the late 1870s, and although at first some look very similar, individual makers can be identified by factors such as the shape of the pillars, the brackets

ABOVE **From the detail of this J. Collinson & Sons of England horse, you can see the very plain, square pillar with the diamond-shaped piece of wood covering the nails on the pillar. This** diamond is seen on other makers' horses, and it is not, therefore, an accurate means of verifying a horse's origin. Note, too, the flat legs typical of Collinson and the slotted hoof.

BELOW **Pillar detail from a Lines Bros. Tri-ang "Sporty Boy" horse, made in 1925.** *(Stevenson Brothers, Kent, England)*

LEFT **A rare cantilever horse made in France c.1900. The design is based on the original patent by Andrew Christian.** (*Musée du Jouets, Poissy, France*)

ABOVE **A painted eye on a 19th-century American horse.**

and fixings used to hold the swing irons, and the contours on the ends of the hoof rails, stand base, and top.

Most manufacturers varied and improved details of their manufacturing processes from time to time, and progressive mechanization sometimes meant less detailed work on parts such as the legs, bodies, and safety stand pillars, which were mass-produced instead of being hand-worked.

Spring horses range from those with a cantilever mechanism to those with single coiled springs. They were at their most popular around the 1920s, although some contemporary makers of fiberglass horses use spring mechanisms. Old spring horses, such as those made by Andrew Christian, were expensive, so there are not many around.

Old horses occasionally become detached from their stands, making it difficult to determine their original mountings, so remember that horses on bow rockers have more stretched-out legs to accommodate the bows, while the angle between the chest and legs is much greater on horses on safety stands.

## EARS, EYES AND TEETH

Specific features need to be examined when you are tracing the bloodline of your old horse. For instance, the ears of late 18th- and early 19th-century horses were very small, increasing to average size by the mid-19th century, and changing to larger, well-

ABOVE **The finely detailed eye painting around the glass eye on a Baby Carriages Ltd. rocking horse.**

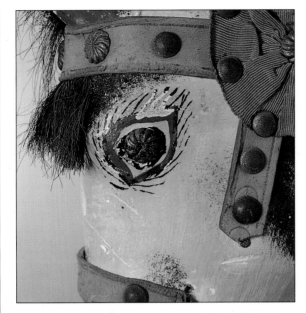

ABOVE **A brass "stud" eye on a J. Collinson & Sons horse. Note the red outline** that is typical of this firm's horses.

## HOOVES

The fixing of hooves on safety stands varies, too. Sometimes they were rabbeted and bolted; sometimes they were just bolted on. Two, three, or four legs might be attached; on fast-moving horses like gallopers and on horses on Jubilee stands, none were. Notice the angle of the hooves – on really old horses they were not angled backward as they are when galloping in real life.

If you are ever in any doubt about the date of a horse which you suspect to have been made before 1880, look at the hooves. Before this date the hooves did not have rabbets because they did not sit partly on top of the rockers but were bolted to the sides. The bolts are almost certain to have become twisted and bent.

East European horses stand out because the manufacturers seemed to have trouble with hooves; one often sees carthorse hooves on racing bodies, and sometimes no hooves at all!

## SADDLES

Except for very small rocking horses, all the old horses made up to the early 20th century had wooden backrests to the saddles. Flattened half-moon-shaped pieces of wood were inserted across the back of the horse at the back of the saddle just in front of the hip. This piece of wood was flush with the horse's hips on each side and curved up in the middle, being held in position with two large screws or nails. It was made of hardwood, with the grain of the wood along the length of the backrest.

Consider the style of the saddle on a horse because this often reflected the country of origin. In real life British saddles are vastly different from North American Western-style saddles. Highly ornate Spanish saddles were common in Mexico and the southern states of the United States.

carved and elegant shapes by the turn of the 20th century. They were reduced to average size in the 1920s and 1930s. Ears on horses from the 1960s onward do not have a lot of shape because they were mass-produced. Nowadays, of course, modern makers produce all sizes.

Information can be gleaned from the eyes of the horse. Old horses always had clear glass eyes with a black pupil, the socket beneath being painted red that showed through. This paint has often peeled away, even though the eye had not been disturbed. The eyes on horses dating from 1940 have the brown color in the glass itself. Dome-headed upholstery nails and sometimes painted nails were used on cheaper models and smaller horses for example J. Collinson & Sons horses (see above) and sometimes Baby Carriage's horses had brass "stud" eyes.

Patricia Mullins discovered that the horses of two Australian makers have unusual features: Roebuck horses had separate teeth glued in, and the heads on Lou Peets's horses always turned to the left, never to the right.

Although most rocking horses, especially those at the lower end of the market, had fixed saddles, some superior Victorian versions had removable saddles modeled on real ones, so that the young riders could learn the rudiments of tacking up.

Before the 1920s all saddles were made of leather and padded with horsehair for quality horses and cotton waste for standard ones. The 1920s and 1930s saw the introduction of Rexine, a synthetic leather using cloth as a base. In the 1960s plastic-coated cloth and corduroy appeared, but watch out – if the original was Rexine, it might have been renewed and the horse might still be an old one.

Early saddle cloths were made of worsted wool or felt, usually in blue or red with decorative braid or fringe around the edge. The shape was roughly oblong, with the bottom back corner elongated to make it more stylish, as in the shape favored for numnahs of the officers' cavalry horses during the 19th century. However, of all rocking horse accessories, saddle cloths are the most perishable and are rarely original they are, therefore, of little use in tracing origins.

ABOVE **A red chest rosette from a recent J. Collinson & Sons horse. Notice how little the style has changed.**

ABOVE **Chest rosette from an old Baby Carriages Ltd. horse on which you can just discern the blue color. Irish craftworkers recognized blue as a winning color.**

## ROSETTES

Surprisingly, vestiges of old rosettes are much more commonly found, sometimes trapped beneath the nails that secured them. Although colors for rosettes in the early 20th century became quite varied, they were originally intended to signify show ring winners, and international horse shows used different colors. In Britain, only at Olympia was a blue rosette the highest award, the rest were red, although in Ireland, America, and Australia blue was the winning color.

Rosettes were sometimes made of leather for durability, and some pre-1930 horses even bore fancy brass rosettes. Although they were later made in bulk and used by many manufacturers, the work of some early makers can be identified by the type of pattern on the rosette nails.

## TACK

Braided bridle straps were more common on the European continent than in Britain. Leather was commonly used until the introduction of cheaper substitutes.

Inferior wood will split or move, especially if it is exposed to direct sunlight and heat. In addition to the effect of the Australian climate, the type of wood used may have tended to shrink, and this may have been the reason for the design of Roebuck's harnesses, which had extra straps at the tops of the legs and neck to cover wood joints.

Except for a few types in the 1930s and on horses manufactured since 1960, the bit and the two rings attached were of painted iron. The bit was of thick, stiff wire which went through the gap at the back of the mouth and was looped around a ring at each side of the mouth. The rings often had two spikes with rounded ends attached, similar to a real horse's bit. They were painted black or silver.

# MANUFACTURER'S MARKS

Manufacturers' marks vary in the form they take. Some are stenciled on the horse or the stand, while only a paper label was affixed on other horses. Sometimes the only clue to the maker comes from initials cast into metal brackets on safety rocking horses which, to make it even more difficult, can be found impressed underneath the two cast-iron brackets at the ends of the stands! In other cases, only the name of the model itself is to be found. The list below includes some names used by manufacturers.

**Alpha Rocker** Fiberglass horse from J. K. Farnell, London, UK, 1962 onward.

**Caledonia** On a brass plate on the chests of G. & J. Lines's horses, 1900–10.

**Charger** Horse with lifelike movements of head and tail, manufactured by Lord Roberts' Memorial Workshops of London, UK, 1920.

**Childtern** H. G. Stone & Co., London, UK, 1920s–1930s.

**Collinson** Collinson & Sons, England. Only horses marked after 1981 have maker's name on gold plate on front of stand base; nothing on pre-1981 horses.

**Come On Steve** Horse based on newspaper cartoon by Bournemouth Novelty Works, Dorset, UK, 1937.

**Cyclops** Australia: pre-1950 Cyclops Toys, post-1950 Cyclops Lines.

**Darenta** Trademark of Vickers Ltd., London, UK.

**Dizzy** Trade name for walking rocking horse manufactured by Whiley Bros of Surrey, UK, c.1947.

**Fadap** (Fabrique d'Aminaux en Peluche), Lang, France, plush-covered horses and donkeys on metal rockers, wheels and tricycles, 1924–78.

**G. & J. L. Ld** G. & J. Lines Ltd, UK, dating from after the time the company became limited, c.1910. Sometimes includes a number denoting size of horse – No. 1, No. 2, and so on.

**Galloper** Name for three-legged rocking horse patented by Tan-Sad Ltd. of Birmingham, UK, 1933.

**Galloping Gee-Gee** Push-along wheel and horse manufactured by Lord Roberts' Memorial Workshops of London, UK, c.1915. Also self-propelled wooden stool horse by Ellis & Co. Ltd. of Wales, c.1918.

**Galloping Gus** Dean's Rag Book Co. Ltd., London, UK, 1927.

**Gee-Gee Kar** and **Gee-Gee Toddler** Trade names for toys made by Montil Manufacturing Co., Birmingham, UK, c.1931.

**Gee-Whiz-Gee** Stool horse manufactured by Lord Roberts' Memorial Workshops of London, UK, c.1915.

**Gesgo** Germany: Gebrüder Schmohl, until 1929.

**Gy-Gy and pony's head** Guy Grelety, 1950 to the present. Won "Oscar" award of French toy industry for show-jumping pony. Makes pastel-painted wooden cutout horses and plush-covered stuffed horses.

**Hercules** Name of line of plush toys on wheels and small rocking horses on wheeled platform on bow rocker made around 1919 by Wholesale Toy Co., London, UK.

**Jubilee** Name of horse on new safety stand made by G. & J. Lines, UK, c.1902–11.

**Jukka** Finland: Jussila Co., Juho, birchwood horses painted or natural in two sizes. Present trademark Jukka, 1923 to the present.

**Keinahoben** Finland: Paulina and Kaija Aarikka, 1984 to the present.

**Kelo** Trade name for tubular rocking horses marketed by Keith Lowe Engineers Ltd. of Yorkshire, UK, 1963-70.

**Les Anes Galopeurs** French, sold by Samaritaine store in Paris, c.1913.

**Lotte** Denmark: K. E. Mathiasen, trademark Lotte, 1975 to the present.

**Mobo** D. Sebel & Co. Ltd. of Kent, UK. Mobo toy marks varied: sometimes a transfer; as part of the overall steel pressing; molded into rubber or printed on to paintwork. "Broncos" carried transfers on their chests (sometimes painted over on old ones), and the word Mobo was pressed into the pedals. "Made in England" may be found on the girth of horses with Bronco-shaped body, but early examples will not have this mark. Later Mobo Pony Express toys had rubber molded pedals with Mobo on. Sometimes small makers' marks are found behind the seats.

**Mournful Mike** Name of toy horse patented by W. H. Jones of London, UK, 1927.

**NB** Belgium, Nazaire Beeusaert, 1930–90.

**Pablo** Merrythought Ltd., UK, 1938 to the present.

**Pampo** N. Clerc et Fils, French, 1900–30s.

**Pancho** Trade name for walking rocking horse manufactured by Whiley Bros, Surrey, UK, c.1947.

**Panurge Pets** H. G. Stone & Co., London, UK, 1920–30s.

**Philo** Trademark of Phillippeau, France, 1951; horses and donkeys in lacquered wood.

**Poni** Finland: Paulina and Kaija Aarikka, 1984 to the present.

**Rajah** Name on horse tricycles manufactured by Cartwright & Co., Birmingham, UK, 1896–1956.

**Ray Delphi** Label used on horses by Harry Field, London, UK, 1973–79.

**Rocking Dobbin** Tubular frame with horse's head produced by Tan-Sad Ltd., Birmingham, UK, 1958.

**Ruedi-Rossli** Switzerland: Rudolf Würgler, 1986 to the present.

**Snaiflex** Trademark of Pintel, Paris, 1920–63. Wide range of plush animals on metal rockers.

**Stag** Brand name of beech horses made by Popes of Hampshire, UK, c.1927.

**Steiff** From the end of 1904 toys tagged with a button in the ear. Early metal buttons embossed with elephant trademark, but in 1905 replaced by buttons with the word Steiff. Paper tags carrying a product number attached to the ear with the button were introduced in 1908–9. After 1926 a paper disk supplemented button identification. Disks attached to the chests carried the name of the animal with bear's head Steiff

trademark. Metal wheels were impressed with company name on outside of the hubs. Later rubber-tired wheels have name on inside of rims. White-tired wheels from 1950s and 1960s have name on outside of wheel rims.

**Stevenson Bros** Brass plate with unique number on stand or rocker of each horse, 1982 onward.

**Swallow** Trademark of Woodrow & Co. Ltd, London, UK, 1933-50s.

**Tally-Ho** Adam's invention marketed by Gamages, London, UK, 1913.

**Thistle** Chest-plate medallion introduced in 1910 by G. & J. Lines of London, UK.

**Tipperary Tim** Name for pedal-driven horse by Tan-Sad Ltd., Birmingham, UK, 1928.

**Toyzona** Trade name for horses by Renisonat Ltd., London, UK, 1919.

**Tri-ang** Lines Bros, UK. Circular green disk with red triangle on it until 1927. Red, gold, and black transfer appeared after 1927.

**Trisky Trike** Trade name for toy horse on three wheels produced by Tan-Sad Ltd., Birmingham, UK, 1927.

**Trojan Horse** Sykes & Co. Ltd., Yorkshire, UK, 1938.

**Troyhorse** Name for horse patented by Troy Toy Manufacturing Co. Ltd., London, UK, c.1935.

**Victory Glider** Trade name of tricycle horse made by Lewis Spencer, Manchester, UK, 1915–30.

**Victory-Nelson** Trademark of Fryer & Co. (Nelson) Ltd, Lancashire, UK, 1946.

**Vilac** Trademark of Villet Frères, Moirans-en-Montagne, France, 1939 to the present. Current horses are called Stormy and are painted or lacquered wood.

**"W" "3" "F"** Wilson & Sons Ltd of Leeds, UK; mark found under stand brackets.

**Yam** Trademark of Cornu of Romainville, Seine, France, 1887. Made wooden horses and other rocking animals until 1968. Taken over by plastics firm in 1963.

# RESTORING

Before you make any kind of replacement for an old rocking horse, it is important to think carefully about your ultimate intention. Do you want your old horse to retain its value? Or perhaps you want it to be just as it was when it was new? Or do you merely want it to be functional again? The answers to these questions determine whether, how, and by whom the horse is repaired or altered.

Most old horses fall into two categories: those that are meant to be looked at and those that are going to be ridden. Very old horses, that is to say those dating from the early to mid-19th century, should be protected against the rigors of use because of their antique value.

When an old horse comes into your possession, you have three choices – conservation, restoration, or renovation. If it is a horse in mint condition, you may decide to conserve it; and this, incidentally, will mean that it will inevitably increase in value as time goes by. Sometimes, however, an old rocking horse is in such a bad state that it is beyond conservation. Modern restorers are familiar with collectors bringing in horses in advanced states of dilapidation. Some of these are in such extremely

OPPOSITE AND ABOVE **A large Lines Bros. horse in Stevenson Brothers** **workshop before and after restoration.**

ABOVE AND TOP **A late
19th-century Ayres horse
with basket seats, before and**

**after restoration carried out
by John and Dorothy Woods.**

poor condition that it would seem they are totally
beyond recall. One such horse was brought into the
Stevenson Brothers workshop in Kent, Britain, in an
assortment of plastic sacks, having been rescued by
an avid collector from a derelict cellar. Obviously in
this case conservation was out of the question, but,
having identified it as an old Ayres horse from the
carving style and the few rusted square-headed nails
lodged in the wood, the Stevensons resurrected it.
They rebuilt the horse from the collection of parts,
made good splits in the wood, replaced an ear here,
a nostril there, rebuilt all four legs from templates
made using what was left of the originals, and
mounted it on carefully fashioned replicas of the
original bow rocker. The result was a perfectly

restored horse ready to be carefully preserved or put
back into service. In fact, that particular horse was
destined to be ridden again by the collector's
grandchildren.

There is an enormous satisfaction to be gained
from restoring an old horse like this to its original
condition and adding it to your collection. However,
if the horse is to retain any historical and antique
value, such restoration should be undertaken only
by a professional. Make sure they really are
professional – a lot of new rocking-horse makers
have been known to jump on the restoration
bandwagon without having developed an eye for the
quality and beauty of rocking horses of old. Insist on
seeing examples of their work first so that you don't
run the risk of having your treasured horse ruined. It
is not unknown for a self-styled restorer to renovate
rather than restore, to the point where the modern
glossy finish can be mistaken for plastic!

Bear in mind that very old horses dating from the
19th century and earlier will be considered for
addition to museum collections to serve as a
historical record for future generations, but only if
they are in original condition. It is important,
therefore, to seek expert advice before restoring an
old horse. Many a museum curator can relate sad
tales of the harm done by enthusiastic amateurs.

If you have found a jaunty little horse made by an
unknown, probably amateur maker, that is the worse
for wear, it would be appropriate to renovate rather
than attempt to restore or conserve. A rocking horse
like this will have started out as a child's toy and will
inevitably have had rough treatment. Splits and
cracks in the wood can be filled with plastic wood
and any broken parts replaced.

If you intend to renew the dapple on a rocking
horse, first prepare the wood by stripping off the old
paint, then sand and prime it. Afterwards paint it
with blue-gray paint. Apply dappling to the rump,
belly, shoulder, neck, and cheeks by stippling the

perimeter of a circular outline. The dapples on the cheeks are smaller than those on the rest of the body. A common mistake is to dab on a series of black spots. The easiest place to start is on the rump. If you are unhappy with your first attempts, just paint over with base paint and start again.

The most vulnerable parts of a rocking horse will always be the mane and tail, subjected as they are by small owners to pulling, tugging, and even haircuts! Where there is a slot on the neck for a mane, you can replace it with a variety of materials, such as hair, yarn, or nylon.

A new hair mane is usually attached to a weft, which should be the same length as the slot. If not, trim it to fit the slot exactly. Put a little wood glue down the length of the slot, spreading it up the sides so that they are well coated. Then fit the weft, resisting the temptation to tug the mane before the glue has set. This will ensure that the mane is held securely enough to resist subsequent tugging from small fingers, but not so tightly that it cannot be replaced at a later date if necessary.

Traditionally, horses are mounted from the left, so manes cascade to the right. When you first put in a new hair mane, it can look a bit unruly; but when the glue sets, you can brush it with a stiff brush so that it will fall naturally to the right side of the neck.

After the mane and tail, the tack of a rocking horse is the next part to deteriorate. Most modern rocking-horse makers can supply tack, and this is your best option unless you have some experience in leatherwork or saddlery.

Stirrup straps come with the saddles and are attached according to the way the horse has been built. If an old saddle is to be renovated, the best way is to take it apart carefully (noting its construction) and use the pieces as a template for the new saddle. On each side of the horse, there is usually a staple in a recess in the wood to hold the stirrup straps. Where these are missing, you will

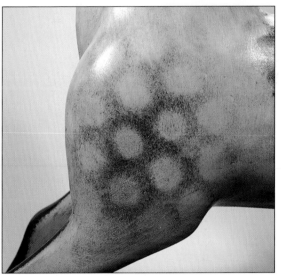

**ABOVE AND TOP** The pattern is actually one light area surrounded by six light areas. The basic pattern is put down first and then expanded in such a way that any of the circles can become the middle one.

have to suspend the stirrup straps over the body of the horse under the saddle. After you have tacked up the horse, you can conceal the tacks used for fixing by fitting antiqued brass studs, placing them so that they cover the tacks.

Repairing an old horse like this can be great fun, but do your utmost to trace the rocking horse's bloodline first, in case you are doing the equivalent of painting a mustache on the Mona Lisa!

# TACKING A ROCKING HORSE

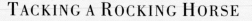

**1** To attach a new tail, put glue in the tail hole. While it is still wet, put some glue on the end of a sharpened dowel, separate the hairs, and hammer the peg into the center of the tail hole through the hair. Leave about ½ inch of the peg sticking out and arrange the hair around the peg. This should hold it firm against any child who feels the urge to pull the horse's tail!

**2** The position of the harness on the horse.

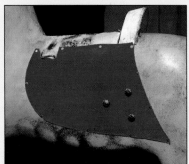

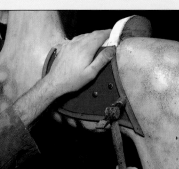

**3** Place one of the parts of the saddle blanket on the side of the horse, pulling it taut so that there are no creases in it and covering up the stirrup-strap staple, if there is one. Then attach it with tacks, molding it to the body of the horse.

**4** You can put a decorative finish on the saddle blanket by tacking a thin strip of braid or leather around the edge.

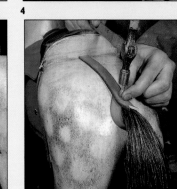

**5** If your horse has a stirrup-strap staple, cut through the blanket with a craft knife to reveal the staple. Thread the stirrup strap through the stirrup iron and then up through the staple before fastening the buckles. Tack down the edges of the saddle blanket around the hole.

**6** Tack on the chest and tail straps as shown here. The tail strap is not just decorative – it holds the tail up at a jaunty angle and protects it from small pulling fingers.

**7** The bridle and reins are placed on the horse as shown in this photograph.

**8** The final step! Tack on a rosette where the chest strap ends meet in the middle of the chest. You can use rosette nails or a ribbon rosette.

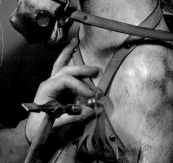

# USEFUL ADDRESSES

**AMERICA**

Abby Aldrich Rockefeller Folk Art Center, Colonial Williamsburg Foundation, Drawer C, Williamsburg, VA 23185

The Essex Institute, 132 Essex Street, Salem, MA 01970

New England Carousel Museum, 95 Riverside Avenue, Bristol, CT 06010

Shelburne Museum, Shelburne, VT 05482

The Strong Museum, 1 Manhattan Square, Rochester, NY 14607

**AUSTRIA**

Tiroler Volkskunstmuseum, Universitatstrasse 2, A6020 Innsbruck

Salzburg Carolina Museum, Salzburg

**BELGIUM**

Museum Voor Volkskunde, Draanlei 65, B-9000 Gent

**BRITAIN**

Lynn Museum, Kings Lynn, Norfolk

Pollock's Toy Museum, 1 Scala Street, London W1P 1LT

**CANADA**

Prince Edward Island Museum, 2 Kent Street, Charlottetown, PE CIA 1M6

**FRANCE**

Musée des Arts Décoratifs, Pavillon de Marsan, 107 Rue de Rivoli, F-75001 Paris

Musée de Jouets, 2 Enclos de l'Abbaye 78300 Poissy

**SWITZERLAND**

Historisches Museum Basel, Steinberg 4, CH-4051 Basel

# SOME MAKERS AND RESTORERS

**AMERICA**

The Rocking Horse Gallery, 803 Caroline Street, Fredericksburg, VA 22401

Red Walsh, 10225 HWY. 50 E, Carson City, NV 89701

**AUSTRALIA**

Equine Manufacturing, D. Reiss, Muttumbeena Victoria 3163

A Griffiths, Hendon, SA 5014

Heirloom Rocking Horses, L & B Koelink, Kilaben Bay, NSW 2283

**BRITAIN**

David and Noreen Kiss, Ashfield House, The Foxholes, Wem, Shropshire SY4 5UJ

Anthony and Pat Dew, The Rocking Horse Shop, Fangfoss, Yorks YO4 5QH

Merrythought Ltd, Ironbridge, Telford, Shropshire TF8 7NJ

Robert Mullis, 55 Berkeley Road, Wroughton, Swindon, Wiltshire SN4 9BN

Stevenson Brothers, The Workshop, Ashford Road, Bethersdon, Ashford, Kent TN26 3AP

John and Dorothy Woods, 180 Chorley Road, Westhoughton, Bolton BL5 3PN

# BIBLIOGRAPHY

**MULLINS, P.** *The Rocking Horse.* New Cavendish Books, 1992.

**FAWDRY, M.** *An International Survey of Rocking Horse Manufacture.* New Cavendish Books, 1986.

**FAWDRY, M.** *English Rocking Horses.* Pollock's Toy Theatres, 1986.

**DINGER, C.** *The Art of the Carousel.* Carousel Art, Inc., 1984.

**SPENCER, M.** *Rocking Horses.* The Crowood Press, 1991.

**INGRAM, D.** *Mr Gamages's Great Toy Bazaar 1902–1906.* Hastings House Publishers, Inc.

*Der Universal Spielwaren Katalog – German Toys 1924–1906.* Hobby House Press, 1985.

# INDEX